Fundamental aspects of legal, ethical and professional issues in nursing

3rd edition

by

Sally Carvalho, Maggie Reeves and Jacquie Orford

Quay Books Division, MA Healthcare Ltd, St Jude's Church, Dulwich Road,
London SE24 0PB

British Library Cataloguing-in-Publication Data
A catalogue record is available for this book

© MA Healthcare Limited 2017
1st edition printed 2002
2nd edition printed 2011

ISBN-13: 978-1-85642-511-7

Cover design by Alison Coombes, Fonthill Ltd

Printed by Mimeo, Huntingdon, Cambridgeshire

Contents

Foreword

Being or studying to become a nurse can be a daunting challenge. There is just so much to consider, and so many different perspectives to balance.

Given all the uncertainties, it can be very tempting to pick up a rule book – the law, a Code of Practice, or a values statement, for example – and point to a section that seems to support your decision. Sometimes this will be enough, but mostly this strategy will fail to take sufficient account of the complexity and richness of daily nursing practice. As the authors rightly point out; in reality, legal, professional and ethical concepts are bound together like plaited hair. They also explain that values are fluid, Codes change, apparently new slogans like the 6Cs become popular and then go out of fashion – and in the end there is so much law, so many ethical principles and professional duties that it can seem impossible to use them to support sensible decision-making, because in practice they just don't fit together.

In the midst of such potential chaos, how can nurses make the best possible decisions each working day?

The authors advise paying close attention to the current NMC Code and the laws of the land, but more importantly they say that it is vital that nurses try to understand their own values and those of others, for it is only by looking honestly at what drives us that we can arrive at the most workable and thoughtful decisions.

For a nurse looking for certainty this may not at first seem like the best news: how can she possibly think so deeply throughout her routine day? But in fact it is a liberating insight: there are rarely absolutely right answers in ethics, no-one gets it perfect always (in truth, most people muddle through most of the time) and so long as you can show that you have considered at least some of the evidence, context, law and preferences in any situation, you will have done well enough.

The message I take from this book is that while there is guidance in law and professional practice, in the end the world is too complicated and uncertain to rely on this alone. It is only by recognising this that you can become the best nurse you can be.

I think the authors' most important observation is that few if any human beings are consistent in our beliefs and actions, and it is a big mistake to imagine we are. Of course, we tend to believe we hold particular values consistently – perhaps 'being honest', 'supporting others' decisions' and 'being respectful' – but sooner or later circumstances occur when these values become so difficult to apply that we do the opposite.

My partner – Vanessa – is resolute in the values she believes in, but one day was surprised to find that she was completely contradicting what she thought was her fundamental preference: the right to know – to be informed in order to make your own choices. As a nurse these values are quite basic to her philosophy of care, but as a mother it turned out that in some circumstances they can swiftly be ditched. We were on an Air Malaysia flight travelling from Kuala Lumpur to London, when one of the engines began to leak fuel. The captain explained that we would have to return and land in Kuala Lumpur, but first we needed to circle for an hour or so in order to ditch fuel so that we could land safely. Vanessa's son, Zak (then 11), was asleep all this time and – in order to protect him – she decided both not to wake him but also not to tell him anything about what was going on, should he wake. She simply could not bear to frighten him or to see him fearful so she withheld the information, in complete contrast with what she supposed her fundamental values were.

Think about your own values – big and small. Look back and see how they have changed as you have changed, and notice too that they have not changed spontaneously, but as the result of the complex backcloth to your life, your growing and the world around you changing and influencing you in fresh ways.

How can knowing this help us make good decisions?

The authors offer various scenarios to reflect on, for example:

'For several days, a 17-year-old patient has refused to eat and drink. When you ask her why, she says it is because of her religious principles.'

They ask you to think about this situation from various angles, because it looks like sooner or later you will have to make a decision: do you allow the patient to starve herself to death or do you try other ways to encourage her – or perhaps ultimately force her - to take food and fluids?

The authors suggest that elements of the NMC Code may be helpful. For example:

Clause 1 - Treat people as individuals and uphold their dignity.

1:3 Avoid making assumptions and recognise diversity and individual choice.

Clause 3 - Make sure that people's physical, social and psychological needs are assessed and responded to.

3:1 Pay special attention to promoting wellbeing, preventing ill health and meeting the changing health and care needs of people in all life stages...

Clause 4 - Act in the best interests of people at all times.

But of course, any thoughtful nurse will notice potential contradictions here, for instance 'respecting the patient's choice' and at the same time 'preventing ill health', so something deeper is eventually required.

This is not the place to explain specifically what this might be, but it is really important to note that the evidence alone – or even the evidence plus Codes plus law – is not always sufficient to make a good decision.

You can think of decisions as if they are bubbles, which pop in and out of existence. All decisions are partly logical and based on evidence, but are also formed from a sea of subtler influences, of which we are mostly unaware: our personalities, our histories, our environment, our culture, our peers, our families and friends, our work pressures and stressors, the political climate, our values – and all these change too. If we want to practice thoughtful health care, then we must always try to see both the logical parts of the decision bubble and the multiple life factors that have brought it into existence.

We can choose to see other people and their decisions positively or negatively, but what is certain is that there are reasons for their choices which – if we and they can comprehend them even just a little better – will help us appreciate them more deeply. We do not have to agree with their decision bubbles just because we may understand their causes a little better. We don't have to respect them and their decisions either. But we can look at them with more awareness, and maybe a bit more sympathy.

And this is the very first thing a good nurse should ask about the 17-year-old who refuses to eat: what factors have caused that decision bubble to bounce into existence? There will be many ways to try to find out, and once things have become clearer it is then possible – although rarely easy – to ask: given what I know about the factors that have caused this decision, how do I support the patient either to sustain it or to make an alternative one? This – coupled with a continuing awareness of your own values – is the true basis of the best nursing care under conditions of uncertainty.

To its credit, this new edition of *Fundamental Aspects of Legal, Professional and Ethical Issues in Nursing* offers many practical signposts to good practice, but does not claim these are always 'the answer'. Taken as a whole, this book shows the way to creative, autonomous, truly professional nursing. Even if different nurses come to different conclusions about the same case, if they have reflected sensitively on both the evidence and the less tangible factors involved, then this is the way good nursing should be.

Professor David Seedhouse
Professor of Values Based Practice
Worcester University

Acknowledgements

We would like to acknowledge the help of the many people who have assisted in the writing of this book.

Firstly, we thank the many students and colleagues with whom we have worked during our nursing and teaching careers. During this time, we have learnt how to answer questions and to find out answers, and to try to give these answers at the level the individual could understand. Students, in particular, have tested us to ensure that they have got the answer to their satisfaction and have challenged us with examples from clinical practice — some of which are included in this book. Without this learning, this book could not have been written.

Secondly, we thank those who have offered advice and information over the years and have contributed to our knowledge. Our specific thanks go to Professor David Seedhouse for writing the Foreword to this edition, and all the other authors acknowledged through the text.

Sally Carvalho, Maggie Reeves and Jacquie Orford

Chronological table of statutes

Offences Against the Person Act 1861

Homicide Act 1957 Suicide Act 1961

Abortion Act 1967

Family Law Reform Act 1969

Misuse of Drugs Act 1971

Health and Safety at Work Act 1974

Nurses, Midwives and Health Visitors Act 1979

Mental Health Act 1983

Public Health (Control of Diseases) Act 1984

Hospital Complaints Procedure Act 1985

Access to Medical Reports Act 1988

Road Traffic Act 1988

Children Act 1989

Computer Misuse Act 1990

Human Fertilisation and Embryology Act 1990

Disability Discrimination Act 1995

Data Protection Act 1998

Human Rights Act 1998

Public Interest Disclosure Act 1998

Health Act 1999

Anti-Terrorism, Crime and Security Act 2001

Health and Social Care Act 2001, 2008, 2012, 2013, 2014

Sexual Offences Act 2003

Children Act 2004

Mental Capacity Act 2005

NHS Act 2006

NHS Redress Act 2006

Safeguarding Vulnerable Groups Act 2006

Mental Health Act 2007

Equity Act 2010

Care Act 2014

Carers Rights Act 2014

Social Action, Responsibility and Heroism Act 2015

Table of cases

Introduction

This book is aimed at those who are new to the fundamental concepts of legal, ethical and professional issues in nursing and who may want help in understanding them. This may be student nurses, when they come across these themes in their pre-registration nursing programme, or qualified nurses who are supervising such students in clinical practice. Hopefully, this book will provide a foundation.

It will look at the three issues – legal, ethical and professional– as separate entities. This is to help the reader understand the concepts in a better way. Although these topics will be looked at separately, in clinical nursing practice they are nearly always combined together. One way of imagining this is to consider a plait of hair. Each of the three strands is separate, but when plaited they are one.

When this occurs in the book, you will see this ✇ symbol:

For the purposes of this text, the term 'patient' will refer to service users as well as patients. The term 'nurse' relates to all fields of nursing and specialist community public health nurses.

Law and ethics are the frameworks within which professional issues are discussed and measured. This does not mean that the law has no morals or there is no law in professional aspects of nursing. They are intertwined.

The Health Service Circular 219.99 (Department of Health, 1999) introduced the requirements for a revised nursing education programme. Under the Nursing and Midwifery Order 2001, the Nursing and Midwifery Council (NMC) is required to establish standards and minimum requirements for pre-registration nursing education. This book will help students to achieve the following NMC (2010) generic competencies for entry to the register.

Competencies for entry to the NMC register

Domain 1: Professional values

All nurses must act first and foremost to care for and safeguard the public. They must practice autonomously and be responsible and accountable for safe, compassionate, person-centred, evidence-based nursing that respects and maintains dignity and human rights. They must show professionalism and integrity and work within recognised professional, ethical and legal frameworks. They must work in partnership with other health and social care professionals and agencies, service users, their carers and families, in all settings, including the community, ensuring that decisions about care are shared (Nursing and Midwifery Council, 2010: 13).

Domain 2: Communication and interpersonal skills

All nurses must use excellent communication and interpersonal skills. Their communications must always be safe, effective, compassionate and respectful. They must communicate effectively using a wide range of strategies and interventions including the effective use of communication technologies. Where people have a disability, nurses must be able to work with service users and others to obtain the information needed to make reasonable adjustments that promote optimum health and enable equal access to services (Nursing and Midwifery Council, 2010: 15).

Domain 3: Nursing practice and decision-making

All nurses must practice autonomously, compassionately, skillfully and safely, and must maintain dignity and promote health and wellbeing. They must assess and meet the full range of essential physical and mental health needs of people of all ages who come into their care. Where necessary they must be able to provide safe and effective immediate care to all people before accessing or referring to specialist services, irrespective of their field of practice. All nurses must also meet more complex and coexisting needs for people in their own nursing field of practice, in any setting, including hospital, community and at home. All practice should be informed by the best available evidence and comply with local and national guidelines. Decision making must be shared with service users, carers and families and informed by critical analysis of a full range of possible interventions, including the use of up-to-date technology. All nurses must also understand how behaviour, culture, socioeconomic and other factors, in the care environment and its location, can affect health, illness, health outcomes and public health priorities, and take this into account in planning and delivering care (Nursing and Midwifery Council, 2010: 17).

Domain 4: Leadership, management and team working

All nurses must be professionally accountable and use clinical governance processes to maintain and improve nursing practice and standards of health care. They must be able to respond autonomously and confidently to planned and uncertain situations, managing themselves and others effectively. They must create and maximise opportunities to improve services. They must also demonstrate the potential to develop further management and leadership skills during their period of preceptorship and beyond (Nursing and Midwifery Council, 2010: 20).

The reader will be invited to cross reference the subjects in this book with all the learning outcomes of the Nursing and Midwifery Council Order (2010) and also The Code (Nursing and Midwifery Council, 2015).

To get the most out of this book we suggest that you have a dedicated notebook/file and, if possible, access to a computer which you will use to undertake the recommended web-based activities to enhance your learning and reflection. These activities are marked with this symbol: ᗩ

This work can then be incorporated into your personal professional profile, which will help you to keep your knowledge and skills up to date throughout your nursing/midwifery career (Nursing and Midwifery Council, 2015).

References

Department of Health (1999) *Health Service Circular HSC 1999/219 Making a Difference: Strengthening the nursing, midwifery and health visiting contribution to health and health care*. Department of Health, London

Nursing and Midwifery Council (2010) *Standards for pre-registration nursing education*. Nursing and Midwifery Council, London

Nursing and Midwifery Council (2015) *The Code: Professional standards of practice and behavior for nurses and midwives*. Nursing and Midwifery Council, London

Nursing and Midwifery Order 2001, SI 2002 No. 253

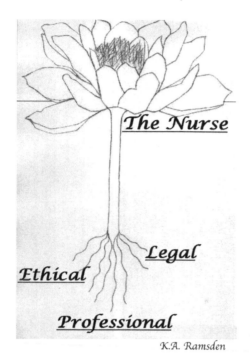

The Nurse

Legal

Ethical

Professional

K.A. Ramsden

The public sees the nurse in full bloom, yet
nurses have their clinical practice firmly rooted
to the legal, ethical and professional foundations
of their education and training (SC)

Section 1

This section introduces some important words and definitions.

- *Chapter 1* considers different aspects of the law.
- *Chapter 2* looks at how nurses behave and perform in practice.
- *Chapter 3* on ethics considers different issues related to conscience.

Although these topics are considered separately, in clinical nursing practice they are nearly always combined together like a plait of hair, as described in the Introduction. The law and ethics are the framework in which professional issues are discussed and measured.

CHAPTER I

What is law?

The aim of this chapter is to ensure that you have a basic understanding of the origin of the law and its relevance to your nursing practice. It covers aspects such as the main categories of law and how they are created. You will be given the opportunity to begin to identify some specific laws that influence nursing and health care.

The term liability is defined, and criminal and civil liability are briefly explained with some comparisons made between the two. Some offences that nurses could commit are identified. The court system is discussed so that you can gain an appreciation of the process in which you or a patient may become involved.

A broad understanding of the law is a requirement of many occupations and members of the public are becoming increasingly aware of their rights in law. Health-care and nursing staff are no exception. The Code (Nursing and Midwifery Council, 2015) makes several references to the law that registered nurses and midwives must uphold. For example, it states that nurses and midwives must keep to all relevant laws about mental capacity that apply in the country in which you are practising; have knowledge of and keep to the relevant laws about protecting and caring for vulnerable people and adhere to laws with respect to medicines management.

Student nurses who are undertaking pre-registration education programmes learn about and have to abide by the standards set by the Nursing and Midwifery Council (NMC) in preparation for becoming registered practitioners. The Code is central to all education programmes, whilst the competencies required by students to enter the register (NMC, 2010) also refer to working within agreed professional, ethical and legal frameworks. Students who fall below the expected standards will be held to account by the appropriate panel or committee within the Approved Education Institution (University) where they are studying towards their field-specific recordable qualification to ascertain their fitness to practice.

Where does law in the UK come from?

For simplicity, the focus here is on England, the primary legislation being formulated in Westminster. The other three countries of the UK share many similarities but there are also some differences and, as a result of legislation in 1998, Scotland and Northern Ireland can now make some laws relevant to their own country. This includes those relating to health issues (Elliott and Quinn, 2010). In Wales the 2011 referendum enables the Welsh Assembly to make legislation in devolved areas which includes health and social care. Later in this chapter you will be able to explore some of these differences yourself, especially if you are practising in these other countries.

There are two main origins of law, one made through Parliament (statutory law) and the other from case law (common law). There are others that are affected by laws laid down in Europe.

- Statutory law has been laid down and passed through Parliament and is often referred to as being 'on the statute book'. It is known as an Act of Parliament and is given a specific title and a date when it has completed the necessary stages.
- Common law has evolved over a considerable period of time and is based upon cases that have set a precedent. The judgments made are often referred to in subsequent cases and act as a 'yardstick' against which future decisions are made. One of the purposes of this is to try and ensure equity in decision making. Common law can be traced back, in some instances, to 12th and 13th century England.

How is statutory law created through Parliament?

There are a series of stages that are followed in both the House of Commons and the House of Lords but they occur at different time intervals. A proposed piece of law may be first introduced in the House of Commons as a Bill. A Member of Parliament (MP), who is often a member of the government of the time, introduces it. There are also Private Members' Bills. These are proposed by backbench MPs who have an interest in a particular subject which they believe should become law. An example is the Assisted Dying Bill presented by Rob Marris MP in 2015 which failed to progress to become law having been rejected in the House of Commons in a free vote of MPs at its second reading (see *Figure 1.1*). A similar fate befell the Abortion Rights Bill in 2006 as a result of deep concerns expressed by the government of the time which did not support the bill. Private Member Bills may be first introduced in either the House of Lords or the House of Commons.

Usually a Green Paper is published and, if the topic is health related, this is distributed for consultation to interested parties, such as NHS trusts or health

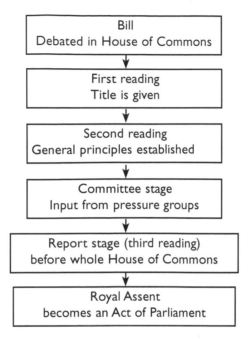

Figure 1.1. The process of creating statutory law.

professional bodies. The Green Paper is often amended as a result of suggestions from a variety of sources, including pressure groups, or even an individual.

A White Paper follows. This sets out what the government intends to do. The subsequent bill goes through a series of readings and stages (*Figure 1.1*), starting by giving it a title followed by an outline of the general principles (second reading). Voting takes place and a majority is needed for progression to the next stage. Once the general principles have been presented a committee is formed which develops these in much more detail. The committee is important because it produces a detailed report for further consideration.

At the report stage, which is debated before the full House of Commons, amendments can be made. Voting occurs and if successful, the process of the three readings is repeated in the House of Lords.

Activity

Make a list of at least five Acts of Parliament that you think are relevant to nursing. Try to include the date that the Act was passed.

Eventually, if both houses are in agreement with all the amendments, the Bill goes to the Monarch for Royal Assent, this signature transforming it to an Act of Parliament. However, the Act does not necessarily come into force (i.e. become law) when the Monarch signs it. Dates are either set in the Act itself or fixed by Statutory Instruments. Interestingly, some Acts have never been brought into force.

This process can be very slow, complex and time-consuming and a Bill may run out of time, never to become law. There are also various delaying tactics that can be employed.

A vast number of Acts affect nursing, hence registered nurses and student nurses should be able to cite several by name and date. Check to see if your list contains any of those listed in *Box 1.1*. The ability to discuss the key aspects and relate them to practice will ensure that nurses do not break the law and will protect the interests of patients and patients.

Box 1.1. Acts of Parliament

- Offences Against the Person Act 1861
- Suicide Act 1961
- Abortion Act 1967
- Misuse of Drugs Act 1971
- Health and Safety at Work Act 1974
- Mental Health Act 1983 (amended 2007)
- Public Health (Control of Diseases) Act 1984
- Children Act 1989 (amended 2004)
- Disability Discrimination Act 1995 (amended 2005)
- Data Protection Act 1998
- Public Interest Disclosure Act 1998
- Human Rights Act 1998
- Sexual Offences Act 2003
- Mental Capacity Act 2005
- National Health Service Act 2006
- Equity Act 2010
- Health and Social Care Act 2012
- Care Act 2014

Legal texts usually contain a table of statutes, if you want to check if there is an Act of Parliament about a particular issue. The important thing to remember is how these statutes affect your nursing practice.

Activity
As there are variations in some statutory laws in Scotland, N. Ireland and Wales look at some of the Acts listed in Box 1.1 in more detail, noting variations that relate to health care, especially if you are practising in any of these countries.

Criminal and civil liability

Activity
Find a definition of liability.
You have probably come up with words such as legal obligation, being answerable for, responsible for …

A crime is a public wrong that is considered unacceptable to society and thus the State prosecutes the offender providing there is sufficient evidence.

The opposite of a public wrong is a private wrong, whereby the offended individual (plaintiff or claimant) sues the wrongdoer in a civil action. The French word tort is often used in relation to these civil cases (Dimond, 2015).

Activity
Try to compare the two types of 'wrong' and make a table of the differences.

In *Table 1.1*, the term R *vs* Another refers to the way a criminal case is named. In this example the Crown Prosecution Service takes the case to court. 'R' refers to Rex (King) or Regina (Queen). 'Another' is the surname of the other party involved, the accused. In civil cases the first name 'One' is that of the claimant while the second 'Other' is the defendant.

The seriousness of criminal and civil cases can vary. For example, a parking offence is a minor criminal offence compared to the extremely serious wrong of negligence. To confuse the issue, some incidents are both criminal offences and civil wrongs, e.g. assault.

In an ideal world, no nurse would ever commit a criminal offence or civil wrong but, unfortunately, some nurses do. The most serious offence would be

Table 1.1. Criminal vs civil liability	
Criminal	*Civil*
Offence against the State	Civil wrong against the individual
May be intentional	Usually unintentional
Prosecuted by CPS: R *vs* Another	Sued One *vs* Other
Proof of guilt beyond all reasonable doubt	Liability on a balance of probabilities
Wide variety of sentences	
Prison, fine, community sentence, absolute discharge	Compensation, payment of damages, apology

murder. Murder is classed as a crime and is a common law offence; there is no such statute as a Murder Act although the Homicide Act of 1957 created amendments which still relate to the trial and punishment of murder today.

Dimond (2015) provides some examples of definitions of certain crimes, such as assault, battery, wounding and theft. She also lists some forms of civil action.

One of the most significant civil offences that may involve nurses is negligence, and this is discussed in *Chapter 6*.

Hierarchy of the courts

There are separate criminal and civil courts in England and most cities have a variety of each. Nearly all criminal cases start out in the Magistrates' Court, which is presided over by lay individuals known as Justices of the Peace (JPs). If the accused pleads guilty to a minor offence, it can be dealt with there. Magistrates have a limited range of sentences they can impose. In other instances the magistrate will hold committal proceedings to decide if the case should go to the Crown Court. There is also a special type of Magistrate's Court known as a Youth Court which deals with young people aged 10–17 years of age.

Activity

Using the information given so far, identify some wrongs that a nurse could commit and classify each as either criminal or civil, and either bound by statutory or common law.

Activity
- Explore the website for the British and Irish Legal Information Institute (www. bailii.org). This website gives many examples of case law.
- To consolidate the information given about the hierarchy of the courts, you might find it helpful to access the structure of the current court system at www.hmcourts-service.gov.uk/aboutus/structure/index.htm

The hierarchy of courts in England is as follows: County Courts and Crown Courts; Divisional Courts; High Courts; Courts of Appeal and the United Kingdom Supreme Court in England. Beyond this are the European Courts. In addition, there is the Coroner's Court that is empowered to investigate deaths which occur under specific circumstances. It functions differently from criminal and civil courts as its purpose is to find out the cause of death, not accuse anyone. Nurses may be required to attend a Coroner's Court as a witness to answer questions if they were involved in the deceased's care.

References

Dimond B (2015) *Legal aspects of nursing*. 7th edn. Pearson Education, Harlow

Elliott C, Quinn F (2010) *English legal system* (11th edn). Longman, Harlow

Nursing and Midwifery Council (2010) *Standards for pre-registration nursing education*. Nursing and Midwifery Council, London

Nursing and Midwifery Council (2015) *The Code: Professional standards of practice and behaviour for nurses and midwives*. Nursing and Midwifery Council, London

Associated study
- You may now want to find out a little more and, apart from the activities suggested so far, you could try to follow an Act of Parliament as it is created, making a few notes in your notebook. Valuable resources are newspapers, television and the Internet. Don't expect it to happen all at once though, remember the legislative process can be very slow!
- If you have ever been called for jury service reflect on what you learned in relation to the areas covered; or follow a case as it is reported in the press or on the Internet.
- Cases that have implications for nurses or health care are, of course, pertinent.

CHAPTER 2

Professional issues

This second chapter in *Section 1* focuses on introducing professional issues.

It starts by asking you to consider the terms professional, professionalisation and professionalism. The history and establishment of nursing's professional body, the Nursing and Midwifery Council (NMC), is discussed. You need to keep updated with the changes that are implemented by the NMC as part of your professional development. An outline of how nursing is controlled and its disciplinary procedures is included.

Professional issues are looked at as a separate subject and are then woven together with legal and ethical issues with examples from nursing practice.

What does professional mean?

Many books have been written discussing the idea of profession, professional, professionalism and professionalisation. What do they all mean?

Activity

Conduct a search to identify a definition for the following words:
Profession, professional, professionalism, professionalisation.

Reading and Webster (2013), Wheeler (2012), Burton and Ormrod (2011), and Tilley and Watson (2008) indicate that a profession:

- Needs a body of specific knowledge based on research
- Has knowledge that is passed on to new entrants to the profession and is guided by members of that profession
- Places the needs of patients before the needs of the professional
- Recognises that accountability for standards is judged by other professionals.

Fletcher and Buka (2007) state that a professional is a practitioner who has undergone a long course of training, the successful completion of which permits him or her to be entered on to a register maintained by the ruling body of that profession. The *Collins English Dictionary* (2003) describes professional as the way a professional behaves; the qualities or typical features of professionals, in other words professionalism. Tschudin (2006) suggests that the term professionalism is not only about what a group of people are, but also what they want to be.

Professionalisation means the process of attaining professional status. The consequence of this according to Rumbold (1999) is that nurses are no longer taught that they are, nor do they see themselves as, doctors' handmaids; they have become independent decision makers.

There are very many different ways of looking at this subject. Many of the books look at the history of nursing, the process of professionalisation and the quest for professionalism. However, most look at the nurse, midwife or specialist community public health nurse as a professional and how they are expected to behave in clinical practice.

The Nursing and Midwifery Council

The United Kingdom Central Council for Nursing, Midwifery and Health Visiting (UKCC) was established following the passing of the Nurses, Midwives and Health Visitors Act in 1979. There have since been amendments to the 1979 Act, notably in 1992 and 1997. It is interesting to note that the professional body here was concerned with the professions identified in its title while the legislation was named after the practitioners. The changes and developments since 1979 have necessitated legislative amendments. Under Section 60 of the Health Act 1999, the Nursing and Midwifery Council (NMC) was created and subsequently replaced the UKCC in 2002.

The NMC governing members are appointed in accordance with the Constitution of the NMC (Schedule 1 of the Nursing and Midwifery Order 2001). The main purpose of the NMC is to protect the public, which it does in a variety of ways, as detailed below.

Register of practitioners

The NMC maintains a register of practitioners and it controls who may or may not be listed on that register. The registration of nurses is not a recent occurrence; nurses were first listed as having been trained to a recognised standard in 1919.

Activity
Search the NMC's website to find out how the members of the Council are appointed. www.nmc.org.uk

The body responsible for this was the General Nursing Council, which functioned up to 1979. There was a similar body which maintained a register of midwives.

Today's register is known as a live register because it lists those who are currently practising, not those who were once nurses and have ceased to practise. To be eligible for entry onto the register the nurse must have successfully completed a programme of education and training, and be of suitable character, usually verified by the university attended. The student will also need to pay the current fee set by the NMC for their initial entry onto the live register

Once on the live register there are requirements that have to be fulfilled by each nurse or midwife; renewal of registration is a requirement every 3 years, as is the payment of an annual fee, along with the completion of the NMC's (2015a) revalidation process which became effective in April 2016.

Activity

Return to the NMC website (www.nmc.org.uk) and read through the Revalidation process; list the eight NMC requirements for successful revalidation.

In addition, anyone can check via the NMC that an individual's registration is current. It is illegal to work as a Registered Nurse or Midwife when one has not qualified or is not included on the NMC's live register.

Although students are not on the register until they have successfully qualified, some of the requirements for renewal of registration form the basis of good practice. Pre-registration students do have to keep a profile or portfolio of their learning and must still keep within the law as indicated in the Code (2015b) which now includes professional guidance for pre-registration students replacing the NMC (2010) guidance.

Education and training standards

The second function of the NMC is in relation to the education and training of nurses and midwives. Universities, NHS trusts and other organisations, such as private nursing homes, HM prison services that provide nurse education, training and/or practice experience, have set standards that students must meet. These are known, respectively, as the Standards for Education and the Standards for Competence, collectively known as the *Standards for Pre-registration Nursing Education* (NMC, 2010). These standards ensure parity throughout the UK for any field of nursing the student is undertaking.

As health needs change so does the role of the nurse, and the standards and requirements of course programmes reflect these.

The history of nursing clearly illustrates the many changes that have occurred since nurse training first began over 100 years ago. It is a long time since nurses were apprentices learning 'on the job', following a medically-orientated model of training culminating in a State final examination. Nurses today undertake a programme of education, use evidence and research as a basis for their practice, and are accountable to their patients, their employer, themselves, the law and the profession.

Standards for conduct and practice

The NMC produces and regularly updates a variety of documents for all nurses. All registered nurses are sent a copy of the NMC Code (NMC, 2015b) when they qualify, and receive new versions when needed or on request. Universities often refer to the Code when teaching pre-registration students, and may require students to access it via the NMC website (www.nmc.org.uk). As the NMC website is accessible to the general public, anyone can obtain a copy of any publication. This is important as it facilitates the accountability of nursing to the public.

The professional body and practitioners regularly review these documents and feedback from the profession is an important contribution in raising standards of conduct and practice. The guidelines also form the basis upon which professional conduct is monitored.

Fitness to practise

The NMC considers and administers procedures related to fitness to practise through one of its statutory committees: the Investigating Committee, the Conduct and Competence Committee and the Health Committee. Each committee is made up of registrants and lay people from outside of the nursing and midwifery professions. If a nurse or midwife is reported to the NMC, an investigation will take place; however, the Professional Standards Authority also has powers to review decisions if they are considered to be too lenient and they will refer these to Court (NMC, 2015c).

Activity

Access the NMC website and access the Investigations Process and the possible Sanctions that can be imposed.

Concerns raised or allegations made about a nurse are investigated by the NMC in which evidence, statements and witnesses are gathered; you may find yourself called to provide a statement or even to attend an NMC hearing to give evidence. The types of allegations investigated by the NMC are:

- Misconduct
- Lack of competence
- Not having the necessary knowledge of English
- Criminal behaviour
- Serious ill health.

This is a formalised professional procedure and the purpose is to obtain information through a Screening Team's processing to prove beyond reasonable doubt that there is a case to answer. The case has to be one that is serious enough to justify removing the practitioner's name from the register. Interim suspension of the nurse may occur if the offence is very serious. Do not forget the main purpose is to protect the public, not to punish practitioners.

However, in response to the Mid Staffordshire scandal where an unusually high mortality rate among patients was identified, the Francis Report (2013), having discovered many professional failings among the staff, recommended that a statutory duty of candour be introduced for health-care providers (recommendation 181). On 1 April 2015 the Health and Social Care Act 2008 was amended to extend a fit and proper person requirement to all providers of health care (Care Quality Commission, 2015). This directly links to the ethical principle of truth-telling (discussed later in this book). This in turn reflects upon a nurse's duty to be vigilant and to have the courage to report concerns about his/her colleagues. Further policy guidance can be found by reading the Freedom to speak up: the raising concerns (whistleblowing) policy for NHS (NHS England, 2016).

Activity

Access the Care Quality Commission (2015) document related to Duty of Candour at: www.cqc.org.uk/sites/default/files/20150327_duty_of_candour_guidance_final.pdf

Following the screening of an allegation or concern and an investigation the following may occur:

- The case may be closed
- The complaint may be referred to the Conduct and Competence Committee for a further formal hearing
- The complaint may be referred to the Health Committee
- Further investigation may take place
- A Notice is sent with detailed charges
- A sanction may be imposed at a Health Committee hearing or a Conduct and Competence Committee hearing.

If the complaint is forwarded for further consideration it is heard in public to reflect the NMC's public accountability. The format of the hearing is similar to a criminal court. The aim is to determine whether the facts are proven and, if this is the case, if it is serious professional misconduct. The NMC has the power to take a variety of actions depending on the outcome of the hearing.

Activity

- Access the NMC website: www.nmc.org.uk and identify what the NMC actions following a hearing for professional misconduct might be.
- Find out how the Health Committee may be involved, how they hear a case and the options open to them.

Your examples will clearly demonstrate the profession's determination to protect the public.

Activity

To summarise answer the following questions. Most of the answers can be found in this text, through your own knowledge or by using the Internet.
- If the NMC Code is a guide or a standard, what purpose does it serve?
- Who is it designed for?
- Who wrote it?
- Name the law that established the body that wrote it.
- What types of issues does it cover?
- What powers does it have?
- What consequences could arise from putting the Code into practice or ignoring its content?

This brings the discussion round to the NMC Code and the other supporting texts regarding medicines, records, and specialist documents for age and client groups published by the NMC to guide and advise nurses who must behave in an appropriate way.

The legal-ethical-professional link

When the NMC Code was written, it was constructed within the laws of England, Wales, Scotland and Northern Ireland. It was based on *ethical* principles and is a *professional* document that adheres to the *law*. A working knowledge of the Code is expected of all nurses by the NMC.

References

Burton R, Ormrod G (2011) *Nursing: transition to professional practice*. Oxford University Press, Oxford

Care Quality Commission (2015) *Regulation 20: Duty of candour- information for providers*. Care Quality Commission, Newcastle upon Tyne

Fletcher L, Buka P (2007) *A legal framework for caring*. 3rd edn. Macmillan, Basingstoke

Francis R (2013) *Report of the Mid Staffordshire NHS Foundation Trust Public Inquiry*. The Stationery Office, London

NHS England (2016) *Freedom to speak up: the raising concerns (whistleblowing) policy for NHS*. NHS England, London

Nursing and Midwifery Council (2010) *Standards for pre-registration nursing education*. Nursing and Midwifery Council, London

Nursing and Midwifery Council (2015a) *Revalidation*. Nursing and Midwifery Council, London

Nursing and Midwifery Council (2015b) *The Code: Professional standards of practice and behaviour for nurses and midwives*. Nursing and Midwifery Council, London

Nursing and Midwifery Council (2015c) *Fitness to practise legislation guidance*. Nursing and Midwifery Council, London

Reading S, Webster B (2013) *Achieving competencies for nursing practice: A handbook for student nurses*. Open University Press, Maidenhead

Rumbold G (1999) *Ethics in nursing practice*. 3rd edn. Baillière Tindall, London

Tilley S, Watson R (2008) *Accountability in nursing and midwifery*. John Wiley & Sons, West Sussex

Tschudin V (2006) *Ethics in nursing: The caring relationship.* 3rd edn. Elsevier, Edinburgh

Wheeler H (2012) *Law, ethics & professional issues for nursing.* Routledge Ltd, Oxon

CHAPTER 3

Values, morals and ethics

Ethics is a subject used every day. You may not identify your decisions as using 'ethics' but, whatever you do in life, there are reasons why you follow certain paths. Over the centuries people have looked at why individuals follow different paths and have considered frameworks to identify trends. This is loosely what ethical theory is. Therefore, literature has been referred to from quite early texts as well as current sources.

Thompson et al (2006) define ethics (which is from the Greek word '*ethos*' – the spirit of a community) as the collective belief-and-value system of any moral community, or social or professional group. It is one of the ways by which a group or community can live in harmony. This definition introduces two more words: 'morals' and 'values'. Again according to Thompson et al (2006), morals and morality refer to the domain of personal values and the rules of behaviour regulating social interactions.

Morality and ethics deal with human relationships – how humans treat other beings so as to promote mutual welfare, growth, creativity and meaning as they strive for good over bad and right over wrong (Thiroux and Krasemann, 2007).

Values are personal and are, according to Simon (1973),

One of a set of personal beliefs and attitudes about the truth, beauty and worth of any thought, object or behaviour. Values are action oriented and give direction and meaning to one's life.

Here is a useful YouTube clip which defines and explains aspects of the above quotation: https://www.youtube.com/watch?v=F7XF6jMsaP0 (Values, Beliefs and Attitudes Definitions - YouTube) - Uploaded by TJunction -16 January 2015. Values are the starting points for morality and ethics.

These three concepts of values, morals and ethics can be seen to interact and relate to each other (*Figure 3.1*). Each person's morals and ethics develop over a lifetime and originate from a variety of things valued. Thus, these values and morals have been acquired from a variety of sources, which will be looked at in this chapter.

These concepts and definitions will now be pulled together to make more sense of them.

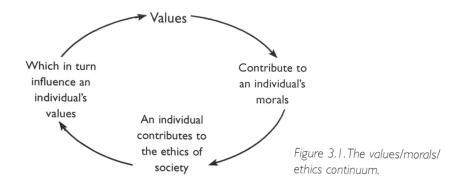

Figure 3.1. The values/morals/ ethics continuum.

What is a value?

Activity

Drawing on your reading and experiences, try to think of a definition of a value and then consider what you value and why.

It is not easy to define exactly what constitutes a value. Perhaps your definition of a value indicates that it is something that is very important to you, it is personal, precious and, very often, is something that you would take risks to defend. Ellis (2015) argues that where there is a mismatch between a person's personal values and behaviours, it can result in stress and tension. However, Ellis (2015) makes an additional comment that if an individual pretends to value – for example – his/her patients or clients, the reality of his/her attitudes will be demonstrated in the type of care he/she will give, as personal and professional values are inseparable.

In an earlier text, Burnard and Chapman (2005) suggest that to find out what a person values and why it is valued, it would be useful to look at anthropology, geography, sociology, psychology and theology, as they relate to that individual.

Activity

How do all these 'ologies' help you decide who or what has influenced what you value?

- Looking at *anthropology* could identify your cultural background and your social situation. Where were you brought up? What was expected of you as a child in different circumstances? What sort of family were you raised in? Apart from your family, who else had influence over you in your childhood?

- *Geography* may identify the environment that you were brought up in and exposed to. What are your attitudes towards conservation, smoking, urban areas, animals, rural areas, beggars, water and sunlight?

- *Sociology* may help you analyse 'why' you value certain things and the influence those around you had or still have on you. Who has influenced you the most throughout your life – particular individuals or groups of people? Do you still value the things that these individuals or groups value? If you no longer value these things, why?

- *Psychology* on the other hand may indicate what sort of person you are and why you respond to external influences as you do. Are you easily persuaded to change your mind? Are you aware of how you tend to respond to different circumstances? Do you find advertising easily or rarely influences you?

- *Theology* may also be a great influence on your value system and be tied up with the other issues considered above. Your spiritual or religious point of view may be the most significant factor of all. When you make a decision does your religious (or other) belief system influence what you do? Do you find you value things that others seem to consider unimportant? Are you conscious of 'trying to do the right thing'? Are your beliefs about 'right' and 'wrong' different from some of your colleagues?

Taking all your answers to the above questions, you may have begun to start thinking about what you actually value and where you first got that notion.

Activity

Here are some other things to consider:
- Decide what it is you actually value – make a list.
- Taking your list put your most important value at the top then prioritise the rest.
- Look back several years and ask yourself if each item on your list was a value then and whether it was as important to you.

Tschudin (2006) and Cuthbert and Quallington (2008) argue that values are not static, they help us to navigate our lives on a personal and professional level, they can also be the means and instruments for making decisions, be ends in themselves and define us as people. Values can be seen as dynamic in that they change and develop throughout life. Not all values are held to be as important as others; there is a tendency to put them into hierarchies.

From a personal perspective a hierarchy of values is where one value is at the top of your priorities and others are of lesser importance. There will be some things on your list that you will never change. They are fundamentally 'you'. From a professional perspective, those readers involved in any type of nursing will need to also consider that, within the Code (NMC, 2015), the professional standards 'Prioritise people', 'Practise effectively', 'Preserve safety' and 'Promote professionalism and trust' give clear guidelines as to how you are required to treat people in your care.

One value that you may never change is that of conscientious objection. Current legislation does permit the nurse or midwife to conscientiously object to providing treatment for patients under Article 4(2) of the Abortion Act 1967 England, Scotland, Wales, and under Article 38(2) of the Human Fertilisation and Embryology Act 1990. If a nurse were to conscientiously object to providing treatment for a patient under the aforementioned legislation, the Code (NMC 2015 Prioritise people 4.4) states:

'tell colleagues, your manager and the person receiving care if you have a conscientious objection to a particular procedure and arrange for a suitably qualified colleague to take over responsibility of that person's care..':

The individual must inform someone in authority if they experience problems that prevent the individual from working within the code or other nationally agreed standards.

The *Janaway v Salford HA [1998]* case clearly defines what constitutes 'treatment' in relation to 'conscientious objection'. This concept relates to issues contrary to your moral beliefs or a strongly held value, such as the sanctity of life, on which you are never prepared to compromise. However, other things will be more flexible and adaptable. For example, do you value your health? Very few people would say 'no' to that question. How do you value your health? could be a more searching question. The following are some of the answers that student nurses have given:

- By not smoking
- By keeping fit
- By eating a healthy diet
- By practising safe sex
- By trying to keep stress free.

Look at one of these answers to see how it could be adapted. Many people aim to eat a healthy diet. Those who truly eat a healthy diet may on occasions eat very unhealthily. This does not mean that they do not value a healthy diet, rather that the individual can be flexible about this particular value.

Another value, such as the sanctity of life, may be more difficult to compromise. This could be an individual's bedrock value that will never change whatever the circumstances.

One of the important things about looking at values is that you clarify for yourself what concepts you value. This clarification can help you understand why another nurse or a patient irritates you. A nursing colleague, for example, may value the concept of 'work' in a different way; a patient may irritate because his or her manners are culturally different from yours. Conversely, your friends may all have the same approach to the balance of academic work and social life (Edwards, 2009). People often make friends with those who share similar values.

As Uustal (1978) warned,

If you do not take time to examine and articulate your values, you will not be fully effective with patients.

This could also relate to your personal relationships.

What you value influences your moral behaviour and the decisions that you make in life. Your values can also be the framework on which you judge others. It is important to remember this when considering the often repeated phrase that nurses must be non-judgemental. Perhaps it is wise to acknowledge that we do judge others but remember that this judgement must not affect the way we nurse. It is what we do with our judgements rather than having them in the first place that matters; how a nurse behaves in a professional manner.

Refer back to *Figure 3.1* and see that although you may have many and varied values, they all contribute to your personal set of morals. Each person has a different set depending on all the 'ologies' referred to earlier. This is highlighted in the Code (NMC, 2015) Prioritise People, specifically items 1, 2 and 4. Your life experiences may also have affected how you react to your past values and those of others. Individually, however, our consciences are sensitive to these values. These values may make you aware of factors that prick your conscience and help you decide the appropriate path.

Activity

Because people are all different, the things that affect your conscience may be different from what affects your friend's conscience. Consider:

- What affects your conscience?
- What helps you decide what is right or wrong?
- What feelings do you experience and what reactions do you receive if you do right or wrong?
- What do you do if someone else takes a different approach to you?

The answers you have given to the questions posed in the box will be very personal, but there will be sentiments that are common to all. Statements like 'feeling guilty', 'feeling uncomfortable with myself', 'angry with myself' and 'worried about what others think' have all been expressed by students in the past. Equally, there are reactions when something felt to be 'right' has been done, feelings of smugness, relief or regret. Other people may not appreciate you 'doing the right thing' because it in turn makes them feel guilty. Their reaction may be one of hostility, rejection or hurt. Such reactions could lead to a confrontation or being ignored. Acceptance of another's viewpoint is not straightforward. If you value something, you will defend it and so will the other person. Responding to this, Ellis (2015) suggests that sharing with others allows us to challenge and test the credibility of our own views.

Relating values and morals to nursing practice

In nursing, as in life in general, you are presented with all sorts of situations to which you will react. Problems come to you that have to be dealt with. The way you deal with each problem will be based on the values that you have and the moral standpoint that you take. Baillie and Black (2015) emphasise that values underpin all aspects of professional practice including decision making, and present some useful activities in their book to help people clarify their moral stance in clinical decisions.

Many of the problems you face have to do with things like honesty, doing good, having a choice, valuing someone's worth and being fair about something.

Philosophers have tried to put these issues into a coherent order. Thiroux and Krasemann (2007) are two such philosophers who have made a simple list of ideas into which values could slot. This list, framework or set of principles provides a way of looking at such issues. They could be quite minor in character or be very weighty issues.

The list consists of the following:

- *The value of life*: Individuals should revere life and accept death
- *Goodness or rightness*: Individuals should promote goodness over badness (sometimes called beneficence), cause no harm or badness (sometimes called non-maleficence), and prevent badness or harm
- *Justice or fairness*: This refers to equality of distribution
- *Honesty or truth-telling*: This includes providing meaningful communication
- *Individual freedom or autonomy*: This includes the freedom of individuals to choose their own ways and means of being moral, within the framework of the above four principles.

When providing health care for patients, pre-registration students in particular, often experience a challenge to their own values when faced with situations that are new and that require them to make decisions that oppose their own beliefs. The Code (NMC, 2015) states in 'Prioritise people' that the nursing and midwifery professions must provide non-discriminatory health care. Therefore, issues such as kindness, dignity, respect and compassion need to be explored in relation to personal and professional values.

Scenarios

Consider each of the following principles and scenarios and work on each scenario using the accompanying questions. Work on your own, or discuss the issues raised with colleagues. They are not presented in the order Thiroux and Krasemann first intended.

Goodness or rightness

A visitor to the ward states that she is the new nurse specialist attached to the ward (she has no identification badge). She wants to see a patient's notes before sorting out discharge requirements with the patient.

- Discuss the principle of goodness or rightness in this situation
- Consider any literature you may find
- Debate alternative strategies you might employ if you were approached by the visitor and the consequences of each
- Which part of the NMC Code is relevant in this scenario?

Justice or fairness

Nurses can often be very short of time. Your ward is very busy and one of your student colleagues is admitted to your ward. You spend quite a long time talking to her. Another patient, who is known by the nursing team for enjoying long conversations because she is normally quite socially isolated, says that she is really lonely and asks you to listen to something that she wants to tell you. You say you are sorry, but you are too busy.

- Discuss the principle of justice or fairness in this situation
- Consider any literature you may find – do not forget other NMC publications
- Debate your reasons for giving preference to one patient and the consequences of this
- Which part of the NMC Code is relevant in this situation?

Truth-telling or honesty

A male patient who is married with a young child is diagnosed as HIV positive. You know from discussions with him that he has other sexual partners. His wife asks you what is wrong with her husband.

- Discuss the principle of truth-telling or honesty in this situation
- Consider any literature you may find

- Debate alternative strategies you might employ if asked this question and the consequences of each
- Which part of the NMC Code is relevant in this situation?

Individual freedom or autonomy

For several days, a 17-year-old patient has refused to eat and drink. When you ask her why, she says it is because of her religious principles.

- Discuss the principle of individual freedom or autonomy in this situation
- Consider any literature you may find
- Debate the different reactions from the people involved in the life of this teenager, and the potential consequences of her decision
- Which part of the NMC Code is relevant in this situation?

You will notice from the questions asked following each scenario that the NMC Code has been referred to on each occasion. This is a deliberate ploy because it is important to be able to use the Code in specific circumstances.

The value of life

ADULT CLIENT: In February 2016, a registered adult nurse was struck off the register by the NMC. The nurse was found guilty of a number of charges, including failing to take and/or record regular observations of a patient after decannulation. The nurse also failed to observe a patient in respiratory distress. In addition she did not assist relatives in repositioning a patient, failed to record nursing care in the records and disposed of a syringe of drugs after an error relating to this had been discovered.

MENTAL HEALTH CLIENT: In February 2016, a registered mental health nurse in Community Health Practice received an interim suspension from the Register by the NMC. This nurse had failed to undertake a risk assessment. He did not check that a home treatment team would be able to provide a client with weekend care. Also, he advised the patient to remain off medication without discussing this with the GP and psychiatrist. He had also failed to note that this client was regularly monitored for side effects/increased symptoms.

CHILDREN'S NURSE: In February 2016, a senior nurse on multiple occasions either failed to complete or even attend working shifts. Because of her seniority she was the one who signed the shift allocation and received payment for shifts not completed. When she applied for another job she failed to disclose that she had been dismissed from her previous position. She was consequently struck off the register by the NMC.

Please choose the scenario which is the most relevant for your field of practice to enable you to:

- Discuss the value of life principle in this situation
- Consider any literature you may find
- Discuss what alternative courses of action the practitioner could have taken to prevent a similar situation
- Which part of the NMC Code is relevant to this scenario?

 Activity

Access the NMC website (www.nmc.org.uk/concerns-nurses-midwives/hearings-and-outcomes/actions-weve-taken/restrictions-and-sanctions-imposed/), look at the latest list and check the reason for being put before the NMC and the results.
October 2015: it is interesting to note the reasons for attending fitness for practice:
Striking off order x 51 people
Fitness to practise changes to the Register x 43
Conditions of practice order x 32
Caution order x 33
The hard facts that have emerged from the review have led to a concerted effort to improve the care to all people accessing health-care services and the changes made, as demonstrated on the next page.

The Francis Inquiry:
Francis Report (2013) watch the interview with Robert Francis giving graphic examples from his inquiry. www.kingsfund.org.uk/projects/francis-inquiry-report?g clid=CLCmsl6L9coCFQjmwgodgH8BeQ

Activity (continued)

From the government's perspective:

A series of measures have been proposed and can be seen in the following link: www.gov.uk/government/publications/2010-to-2015-government-policy-compassionate-care-in-the-nhs

From the nursing perspective:

Cummings and Bennett (2012) write: '…Due to a variety of factors, the last few years have seen many instances of care ranging from excellent to very bad….care that falls short of what they have a right to expect, sometimes by a long way - we will all have seen such care in the course of our working lives.

We know we miss too many opportunities to support people keep well, connected and healthy… society and the health, care and support system is changing fast, and we will need to prepare to meet the changing needs and work in new ways…to tackle some of the issues that emerged from the Compassion in Practice Review, which concluded that…due to many high profile cases of health care professionals failing to meet the standards expected of them, Nursing, Midwifery and Care Staff: our Vision Strategy (2012) was produced via NHS England.' (Cummings and Bennett, 2012)

From these reports and much soul searching, the simple concept of the 6 C's emerged. However simple the concept, the effect on a patient or client can only be classed as right, ethical and good. Below is a link to a useful, wider explanation of the 6 C's, sometimes also called the 'Essential Skills Cluster' www.nhsiq.nhs.uk/media/2592870/6csnursing.pdf

Having looked at this link, there is a distinct emphasis on good communication skills. A really useful book that could complement your communication skills is Pavord and Donnelly (2015) as they explore key concepts including, personal values; understanding ourselves and our impact on others, listening to people, and interpersonal communication. In addition, you may wish to look at the history behind the '6 C's'. Several people were examining the need for a 'care structure' – the different people and their ideas are chronicled in Baillie and Black (2015).

The legal-ethical-professional link

The issues addressed and the possible subsequent questions illustrate the 'plait' referred to in the Introduction. Although legal, ethical and professional issues are separate, in nursing practice they are normally entwined.

Activity

Access the *Values Exchange* developed with Seedhouse (2009) (www.values-exchange.com). This is a decision support programme that will help you to explore your ethical beliefs in relation to a range of scenarios. Access one of the cases and work through it.

References

Baillie L, Black S (2015) *Professional Values in Nursing*. CRC Press, Abingdon

Burnard P, Chapman CM (2005) *Professional and ethical issues in nursing: The Code of professional conduct*. 3rd edn. Baillière Tindall, London

Cummings J, Bennett V (2012) *Compassion in Practice. Nursing, Midwifery and Care Staff Our Vision and Strategy*. Department of Health, NHS Commissioning Board, Leeds

Cuthbert S, Quallington J (2008) *Values for care practice*. Reflect Press Ltd, Exeter

Edwards SD (2009) *Nursing Ethics: A Principle Based Approach*. Palgrave Macmillan, London

Ellis P (2015) *Understanding Ethics for Nursing Students*. Sage, London

Francis R (2013) *Report of the Mid Staffordshire NHS Foundation Trust Public Inquiry*. The Stationery Office, London

Janaway v Salford HA [1988] 3 WLR 1350(HL)

Nursing and Midwifery Council (2015) *The Code: Professional standards of practice and behaviour for nurses and midwives*. Nursing and Midwifery Council, London

Pavord E, Donnelly E (2015) *Communication and Interpersonal Skills*. 2nd edn. Lantern Publishing Ltd, Banbury

Seedhouse D (2009) *Ethics: The heart of health care*. 3rd edn. Wiley-Blackwell, Chichester

Simon SB (1973) Meeting yourself halfway. Cited in: Tschudin V (1992) *Values: A primer for nurses*. Baillière Tindall, London

Thiroux JP, Krasemann KW (2007) *Ethics: Theory and practice*. 9th edn. Prentice Hall, New Jersey

Thompson IE, Melia KM, Boyd KM (2006) *Nursing ethics*. 5th edn. Churchill Livingstone, Edinburgh

Tschudin V (2006) *Ethics in nursing: The caring relationship.* 3rd edn. Elsevier Ltd, Edinburgh (this is a link to a useful first chapter of the book www.mheducation. co.uk/openup/chapters/9780335241651.pdf)

Uustal D (1978) Values clarification in nursing: Application to practice. *American Journal of Nursing* **Dec**: 2053–63

Section 2

In this section you will begin to see how the three strands, legal, ethical and professional introduced in *Section 1*, are plaited together and applied to your practice. The topic areas covered in this section are:

* Responsibility
* Accountability
* Negligence

CHAPTER 4

Responsibility

Some definitions will be looked at first and then you will be asked to identify aspects of your everyday life for which you are responsible. As soon as you start your education and training as a nurse, you begin to be responsible for a variety of things and when you go out into clinical practice, even for the first time, this list grows. Discussion of some of these will help you to understand the implications of accepting responsibility.

As a registered nurse, you are responsible for students you teach and supervise. If you are a clinical mentor and/or assessor for a student your role encompasses more than just responsibility, you are accountable for that student, as will be discussed later in this section.

Activity
• Write a definition for the word 'responsibility'.
• What does responsibility mean to you?

Compare your answers to a selection of definitions provided by other nursing students:

• Liable, dependable
• An obligation, duty
• Being trusted
• Completion of tasks
• Willingness to do something
• Something given to you when you've shown you can do it or have learned it
• Being in charge of a given situation
• Taking charge of expectations
• Standing by what you believe in
• Being aware of and concerned for others.

Some students used phrases like 'being accountable for your actions', 'making intelligent, educated judgements', and 'facing the consequences'. You will see as you progress through *Section 2* that these phrases are more akin to a definition of accountability, so if you wrote similar definitions keep them for later as there is a link between responsibility and accountability.

Cuthbert and Quallington (2008) identify that responsibility relates to accepting a task or duty that you have been given. Thus, there are two components to responsibility: one being asked or charged to do something and the other accepting this task willingly.

Activity

Make a list of things you are responsible for in your everyday life.

It is impossible to give a definitive list as we are all individuals, but your list may contain items such as caring for children, exercising the dog, feeding the cat, taxing and insuring the car, doing the shopping and laundry, and paying household bills.

Activity

Select one task from your list and identify what this responsibility involves and why.

There may be some very sound reasons for undertaking a responsibility. The list below provides some of these.

- The law says you must
- Fear of punishment
- It is the right thing to do – morally, ethically and/or honestly
- It is what is expected by others or society in general
- It may be because you always have done it and are conditioned into doing it without thinking any further.

Responsibility is personal and derives from being a citizen and human being. As a nurse, if you have agreed to undertake a task there is an expectation that you will do it to the best of your ability, safely and correctly. Safety is the required level of ability for students in the early part of the pre-registration course. This requires you to have:

- *Knowledge* of what the task is and why you are doing it
- The *skill* to perform the task
- An appropriate *attitude* to the patient.

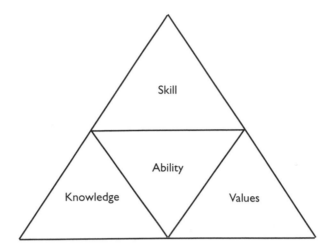

Figure 4.1. Prerequisites for responsibility.

This is likely to include the ability to communicate effectively and demonstrate that you value the patient's individuality, dignity and privacy.

The triangle in *Figure 4.1* illustrates the link between these prerequisites. According to Bergman (1981), ability is one of the preconditions necessary to become firstly responsible and ultimately accountable. You will return to Bergman's work later in this section.

Student nurses' responsibilities

From the first day of any pre-registration course, students take on responsibilities. Attitudes to one's own learning and that of other students are very important. The student is immediately responsible for attending lectures, punctuality, respecting others' desire and need to learn, being committed to and involved in the course, and being self-directed and motivated. Other areas of responsibility require you to act upon advice, guidance and feedback from academic staff and begin to develop your portfolio of learning. These may seem very obvious and are not exclusive to nursing students.

Student nurses are also responsible for their health and are required to have the relevant immunisations and vaccinations before commencing clinical practice. Another important area includes the need for a Disclosure and Barring Service (DBS) to ensure that the student is a suitable person to be caring for others and the student has a responsibility to provide any relevant information relating to this. There are links here again with professional issues because, as you discovered earlier, the Nursing and Midwifery Council (NMC) must ensure that the public is protected, hence there are mandatory sessions that students will have to attend at their university, such as manual handling training.

The list below identifies general areas of responsibility that the student nurse has in relation to the NMC's (2010) Standards for pre-registration nursing education:

- Treat people as individuals
- Respect a person's confidentiality
- Collaborate with those in your care
- Ensure you gain consent
- Maintain clear professional boundaries
- Work as part of a team
- Recognise and work within your limits of competence
- Ensure your skills and knowledge are up to date
- Be open and honest
- Act with integrity
- Protect people from harm
- Uphold the reputation of the nursing and midwifery professions.

Activity

In addition to the above responsibilities, what do you think student nurses will be responsible for on their first clinical placement?

It can be seen that nurses have responsibilities to patients, relatives, colleagues, society and themselves; however, these responsibilities should reflect the level of education and training of the nurse or student (NMC, 2010, 2015).

Responsibility is often linked to roles: different roles have different responsibilities. Compare the responsibilities of students on their first placement with more senior students, or students with registered nurses. Adult field nurses may have different roles from child, mental health or learning disabilities nurses. If you are a clinical mentor, your role will be expanded to encompass this with additional responsibilities.

Activity

The NMC's (2010) Standards for pre-registration nursing education provides a more comprehensive list of pre-registration student responsibilities.

* Access the current guidelines to familiarise yourself with them.

Implications of responsibility

If you refer back to some of the reasons why you undertake the personal responsibilities you listed at the start of this section, the implications of failing to take them show similarities. For example, as a nurse, if your practice contravenes the Health and Safety at Work Act 1974 there may be legal implications for you and/or your employer. If you fail to practise to the standard set by any of the NMC guidelines, a complaint may be made. In the first instance, as a student, this may be to your clinical mentor or clinical manager who may address you and advise you how to improve your practice. Continuing failure to practice appropriately could result in failure to achieve the learning outcomes required by the NMC. This could mean that a student would be unable to continue training.

If there is serious inappropriate behaviour, such as theft or patient abuse, immediate withdrawal from the nurse education and training course is likely, in addition to possible legal consequences.

Registered nurses who fail to practice or behave professionally may be disciplined by the NMC, as described in *Section 1*.

Most nurses, at some time during their careers, experience occasions when their conscience is troubled by aspects of their work or that of others. This can result in feelings of discomfort, anxiety and concern about continuing as a nurse. For students with little experience this can be quite distressing and should be voiced so that they can be supported through such experiences and learn from them. Support is available from clinical mentors, managers, clinical link/liaison teachers, personal tutors and other academic staff as well as other students and nursing colleagues.

 Even when qualified, nurses will often find such support is required. These are ethical issues so, once again, the three strands which form the basis of this text are woven together.

It can be seen that student nurses become responsible very early on and need to understand what this means and entails. The NMC's (2010) guidance on professional conduct for nursing and midwifery students emphasises this important aspect both to protect the public and enhance the profession of nursing.

References

Bergman R (1981) Accountability: Definition and dimension. *International Nursing Review* **28**(2): 53–9

Cuthbert S, Quallington J (2008) *Values for care practice*. Reflect Press Ltd, Exeter

Nursing and Midwifery Council (2010) *Standards for pre-registration nursing education*. Nursing and Midwifery Council, London

Nursing and Midwifery Council (2015) *The Code: Professional standards of practice and behaviour for nurses and midwives*. Nursing and Midwifery Council, London

CHAPTER 5

Accountability

By the end of this chapter you should be able to define accountability and give examples of the origins of accountability with reference to a variety of literature. You should be able to differentiate it from responsibility and identify the prerequisites of accountability. To whom you are accountable will be determined and some aspects of accountability in practice will be discussed. The consequences of accountability in relation to standards of care will be outlined. The Nursing and Midwifery Council (NMC) Code (NMC, 2015) clearly establishes that registered nurses and midwives are accountable for their practice, thus accountability is an integral part of professional practice. What does this mean?

Some of the phrases given by students in *Chapter 4* for responsibility were actually more indicative of accountability. Examples included: making judgements, being called to account and justifying what you did, being answerable for and facing the consequences of one's actions.

Many people confuse responsibility and accountability, perhaps because there are links between them. Responsibility and accountability are closely connected but are not the same, thus they should not be used synonymously. Savage and Moore's (2004) study identified that accountability required further definition among the study's participants.

Bergman (1981) illustrates the links in her model of the preconditions leading to accountability (see *Figure 5.1*).

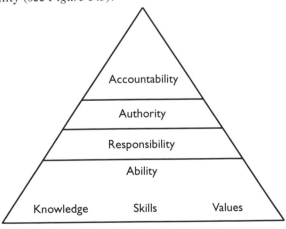

Figure 5.1. Preconditions leading to accountability.

You will remember that the lower levels of this triangle were used when discussing responsibility earlier.

Authority arises from the position you are given and accept, which in turn allows you the power to make decisions. Decision making involves making judgements in a wide variety of circumstances. This suggests that you also need to be autonomous, being given the freedom to make those choices. Walsh (2002) includes this in saying that to be accountable is to have responsibility both to self and others while having the authority to act autonomously. Lewis and Batey (1982) suggest that authority is needed to carry out actions for which you can be held accountable while Pattison (2009) links the degree of accountability to the degree of authority. Cox (2010) suggests that there needs to be a clearer understanding of responsibility and accountability, particularly as the working boundaries of health-care practitioners have shifted so that nurses are working autonomously in areas that were previously the domain of doctors, while health care assistants are assuming responsibilities for activities traditionally performed by registered nurses. The Royal College of Nursing (2015) states that all health service providers are accountable to their employers and must follow their contract of duty and that they are also accountable to the criminal and civil courts. Under the Health Care and Associated Professions (Indemnity Arrangements) Order 2014 it has been a legal requirement for all health-care professionals to hold an appropriate indemnity arrangement, thus it is a mandatory inclusion within The Code (NMC, 2015).

Where does the authority come from?

As a student in the early stages of a nursing programme, authority is given to you by the education and training body, in partnership with the university where you are studying. When you undertake clinical practice it is your clinical mentor who gives you the authority to participate in care delivery. At first this is under supervision but, as you gain experience, authority increases in line with your more senior status. Both responsibility and authority are linked to this developing role where you may be judged as capable of giving some aspects of care unaided. Once qualified the authority is given by the NMC, as part of being on the register, and by your employer within the job description which applies to your post. You are now considered to be accountable.

Professionally, you may delegate responsibility to someone else but not accountability; this remains with the person doing the delegation who must ensure that whoever they ask to undertake a task/duty is able to perform that task/duty correctly. Individuals asked to perform the task/duty must say if they do not feel capable in accordance with the NMC Code (2015). This forms an important part of the relationship between a student nurse and clinical mentor.

Student nurses are never professionally accountable in the same way as registered nurses and the NMC (2015) states that it is the registered nurse with whom you are working who is professionally accountable for the consequences of your actions and omissions during the delegation of tasks/duties. However, as a student you can be called to account by the law or the university who is educating and training you.

To summarise, professional responsibility and accountability are not the same. The key differences are:

- Responsibility has to be accepted
- You can be inexperienced but still have responsibilities, whereas accountability comes with experience
- Responsibility can be delegated but accountability cannot
- Someone must give you authority before you can be accountable
- Accountability requires you to make autonomous decisions
- You must be prepared to answer for your actions to be accountable.

Activity

List who you think the registered nurse is accountable to.

Figure 5.2 illustrates how the law is an integral part of nurses' accountability.

Student nurses who undertake any aspect of care which the mentor is unaware of ('going off on a frolic of their own!') will have put themselves into a position of being accountable.

Student nurses' duties can include what they say, write or do. In the case of what they say, they are accountable because no one else puts words in their mouth. What they write requires countersigning by a registered practitioner so, although they are responsible, the registered nurse is accountable. *Chapter 8* will explore the standards required in relation to written communication.

The same situation arises in relation to what you do, as it should be under supervision or with the knowledge of the mentor who considers you to be competent. This would be in agreement with your own perception since the NMC (2010) indicates that you must seek help from a competent practitioner until you have acquired the requisite knowledge, ability and skill.

Figure 5.2. Spider diagram of nurses' accountability. Adapted from Dimond (2002: 5).

Two expressions are used in relation to accountability – acts of commission and acts of omission. If you provide care that you know is of a poor or incorrect standard, for example, dragging a patient up the bed, this is an act of commission for which you could be held accountable. Although you may have repositioned the patient and made him or her more comfortable the manner in which you did it was unacceptable. You should also consider things not done which should have been done. These are called acts of omission.

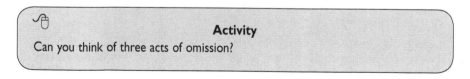

Activity

Can you think of three acts of omission?

Both qualified nurses and students can commit acts of commission and acts of omission.

Acts of omission are often not intentional. However, the consequences for the patient could be serious as you will see later in *Chapter 6* on negligence, as the student is accountable under common law. Nurses are expected to uphold the good standing and reputation of the profession, irrespective of their status.

Answer

- You may have thought of not completing some type of chart, such as an observation or fluid balance chart although you did perform the task.
- Failing to follow a procedure or policy correctly, e.g. not informing a detained mental health patient of his or her rights under the Mental Health Act 1983.
- Not passing on information to the rest of the multidisciplinary team despite the patient giving you permission.
- Not explaining a child's care to a parent.

 Professional accountability incorporates legal, moral and ethical aspects and sets a very high standard for nurses.

The implications of accountability may appear to be similar to those identified at the end of the chapter on responsibility.

The severity of the sanction depends on what you have done but anything that means you cannot continue as a nurse can be catastrophic. Being removed from the register as a result of a criminal conviction or being found guilty of professional misconduct may end the career of a registered nurse. Being dismissed from the course as a student will prevent you from getting on the register in the first place. Sometimes an employer may dismiss you but you may still be able to work elsewhere as a nurse provided that you remain on the professional register. The views of colleagues or your own feelings of disgust or self-hatred can be very hard to deal with and may result in your choosing to leave nursing. Moral and ethical implications can be just as strong as legal or professional sanctions, the latter are simply imposed by someone else.

To help you apply all this to practice try the following activity.

 Activity

Identify the variety of sanctions that could be imposed by the following and explain why

- NMC   • Colleague   • Society   • Employer   • Self

Activity
- Read the following fictional scenarios and decide who you think is responsible and/or accountable.
- Use Bergman's prerequisites of accountability mentioned earlier and think about whether the student should be able to undertake the duty.

Scenario 1

Mary wishes to have a shower and as you helped her to have a bath 2 days ago you feel confident that you are able to do this unsupervised. Mary finishes her shower and asks you to pass her the towel. Unfortunately she drops it on the shower floor where it rapidly becomes too wet to use. 'Don't worry, Mary', you say, 'I'll just pop and get another one, I won't be a minute'. On your return you find Mary unconscious on the floor, half out of the shower. She appears to have tried to step out of the shower to put on her dressing gown.

Scenario 2

You have a very good clinical mentor who has worked with you all morning. Together you have just finished washing an elderly, mentally ill and dependent gentleman. This is a new experience as most of the patients you have met have been self-caring. The gentleman is now comfortably sitting in a chair so your mentor says, 'Just comb his hair and do his mouth and I'll start the drug round, join me when you've finished.' She disappears before you have time to reply. You are aware that this patient has a history of swallowing difficulties and is an epileptic.

Conclusion

However accountability is defined, it is important to remember that the courts are the final venue for the resolution of disputes in medicine and nursing (Pattison, 2009).

References

Bergman R (1981) Accountability: Definition and dimension. *International Nursing Review* **28**(2): 53–9

Cox C (2010) Legal responsibilities of accountability. *Nursing Management* **17**(3): 18–20

Dimond B (2002) *Legal aspects of nursing*. 3rd edn. Longman, Harlow

Health Care and Associated Professions (Indemnity Arrangements) Order 2014

Lewis F, Batey M (1982) Clarifying autonomy and accountability in nursing services. Cited in: Jones M (1996) *Accountability in practice*. Quay Books, Mark Allen Publishing, Salisbury

Nursing and Midwifery Council (2010) *Standards for pre-registration nursing education*. Nursing and Midwifery Council, London

Nursing and Midwifery Council (2015) T*he Code: Professional standards of practice and behavior for nurses and midwives*. Nursing and Midwifery Council, London

Pattison D (2009) *Medical law and ethics*. 2nd edn. Sweet and Maxwell, London

Royal College of Nursing (2015) *Accountability and delegation: A guide for the nursing team*. Royal College of Nursing, London

Savage J, Moore L (2004) *Interpreting accountability: An ethnographic study of practice nurses, accountability and multidisciplinary team decision-making in the context of clinical governance*. Royal College of Nursing, London

Walsh M, ed. (2002) *Watson's clinical nursing and related sciences*. 6th edn. Baillière Tindall, London

CHAPTER 6

Negligence

The first two chapters in this section have focused on professional issues in relation to nursing practice but this final chapter looks at one legal implication of poor practice to complete the picture, that of negligence. Nurses who fail to practice safely or carry out their duties carelessly potentially run the risk of being negligent. Mistakes may not be intentional but failing to meet the standards of practice required can result in harm and may have a devastating effect on patients.

Activity
• Find a legal definition for the word 'negligence'.
• Search for the case *Anderson B in Blyth v Birmingham Waterworks Co* [1856] 11EXCH 781. This case explores issues related to 'negligence'.

Activity
Can you recall what type of 'wrong' negligence is?

In this chapter we will look at some actual cases (which have been simplified for this book) to determine the components that have to be proved by the claimant if he or she is to win the case. Reference is made to professional and other relevant documents that help to set standards of care and that may be used in legal situations.

Activity
To whom does the term 'claimant' refer?

The defendant is either the individual practitioner who is alleged to have caused the harm or the organisation which employs that practitioner. Check back to *Chapter 1* if you have forgotten how this is referred to in most literature. In most cases which involve nurses it is the employer who is taken to court as the purpose of negligence is to sue for compensation and very few nurses would be able to pay if the case is proven. However, it is now a mandatory requirement for all registered nurses and midwives to verify that they have indemnity insurance (Nursing and Midwifery Council (NMC), 2015).

In 2014/15 the NHS in England paid out over £1.1 billion in compensation, one third of which went to lawyers who took on these cases and this is expected to rise to £1.4 billion in 2016. This places increasing pressure on the health service and is of major concern and intense debate. The NHS Redress Act 2006 (England and Wales) sought to provide recipients of NHS care the opportunity to seek redress without having to commence court proceedings. In these situations an ex gratia payment may be made to the claimant without an admission of liability.

Activity

Access the NHS Litigation Authority at www.nhsla.com and compare the number of clinical negligence claims and payments made for 2013/14 and 2014/15

Activity

Access the NHS Redress Act 2006 at www.legislation.gov.uk and identify which claims can be addressed under this legislation.

The reason the employer is identified in negligence cases is because employers take responsibility for the actions of the employee. This is known as the principle of vicarious liability and the employer must be insured against employees' actions which may cause harm to colleagues and/or patients. Vicarious liability only applies if the employee is working within his or her normal employment which is explained in the contract of employment and job description (Fletcher and Buka, 2007). The basis of proof is one of a balance of probabilities, which means that there must be a greater than 50% chance of the act causing or contributing to harm (Moody, 2001) and that there was a failure to follow a reasonable standard of care.

Activity

Follow this link to learn more uk.practicallaw.com/2-500-6576?service=construct (PLC - proof on the balance of probabilities: what this means in practice)

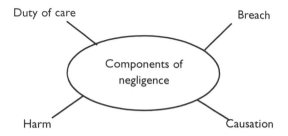

Figure 6.1. Components of negligence.

Harm is one of the four aspects which claimants must prove. These aspects or components of negligence are illustrated in *Figure 6.1*.

Duty of care

One of the main roles of a nurse is to care for patients (NHS England, 2012) and it is not usually difficult for the claimant to prove this if the nurse was on duty and working within the guidelines determined by the employer and profession.

Activity

Find the case of *Donoghue v Stevenson* [1932] AC 562 in any legal text to explore duty of care further to answer the question 'who in law is my neighbour?'

However, if the nurse is off duty the situation is different because legally the nurse does not have a duty to intervene, although professionally, the NMC (2015) stipulates that the nurse should always offer help if an emergency arises in their practice setting or anywhere. However, the NMC (2015) do stipulate clause 15.1 of the Code that the nurse must only act in an emergency within the limits of their knowledge and competence. In the case of, for example, a road accident, then the nurse takes on a legal duty to care for the person appropriately. Hence a duty of care would exist and the expectations of the nurse would be greater than that of the average passer by. Therefore, by attending to an accident victim, a duty of care exists and there is an expectation that the care provided will be of a reasonable standard, i.e. to the best of the nurse's ability and within his/her sphere of competence. In such a case the nurse would be acting legally, but with a professional duty in a voluntarily position as a 'good samaritan' (NMC, 2015). The Social Action, Responsibility and Heroism Act 2015, which applies to England and Wales only, protects volunteers, teachers and organisations from legal action if they act in an emergency. As stated in Chapter 5 of this book, the NMC (2015, 2016) stipulate the requirement for a nurse to have indemnity insurance under the Health and Associated Professions (Indemnity Arrangements) Order 2014.

Breach of duty of care

Rules and regulations are written to both guide and protect and they contribute to the standard of care that a patient may expect from a nurse in a given situation. You should now be aware of the origin of many of these rules and regulations which form professional guidelines, such as the NMC Code (2015).

There are also policies and procedures produced by employers that help determine the standards set, for example, manual handling or infection control policies. You may be able to recall statutory laws that relate to these, such as Health and Safety at Work Act 1974 and the Public Health (Control of Diseases) Act 1984. It is the practitioner's responsibility to find out what the standard is; ignorance is no defence in law. In addition the Department of Health and the National Institute for Health and Care Excellence (NICE) regularly issue benchmarks and protocols which update and guide practice. The nurse therefore has to keep abreast of these and other guidelines to ensure his/her practice is current and evidence-based to minimise the risk of negligence. If a nurse does deviate from accepted practice he/she must justify and record his/her actions (Dimond, 2015).

Despite all this guidance, rules may be broken, either deliberately, when someone takes a 'short cut' perhaps, or unintentionally. In negligence terms, this is a breach in a duty of care. The claimant has to prove what standard of care was required and how it was breached. To assist in this the question of what is reasonable needs to be answered.

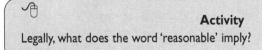

Activity

Legally, what does the word 'reasonable' imply?

The standard or precedence for reasonableness is known as the Bolam test which was set following the legal case of *Bolam v Friern Barnet HMC* [1957] (Dimond, 2015).

Bolam was a patient who was given electroconvulsive therapy (ECT). The practice at that time (1950s) did not usually involve giving a muscle relaxant or anaesthetic. As a result of the treatment, the plaintiff suffered fractures and sued the health authority. Bolam failed to obtain compensation because at the time, this was the accepted procedure and many other doctors in that field followed the same practice. In other words, this was the accepted standard of the day and the actions of the defendant were reasonable under those circumstances.

In the case of a nurse then, the test of reasonableness says that the standard is not that of the highest skilled nurse but of the ordinary skilled nurse who is practising that skill competently.

There have been other precedence cases such as *Whitehouse v Jordan* [1981] (Dimond, 2015) which have added to this question of what is reasonable. In *Whitehouse v Jordan*, although there had been an error of judgement on the part of the obstetrician, he had been acting in a reasonable way.

These two cases highlight the fact that there may be differing bodies of opinion or sound reasons for not adhering to the accepted principles without being found negligent.

Was harm caused?

For a negligence case to be considered by a court the claimant must have been harmed in some way, unlike professional misconduct cases which do not have this requirement. The harm must also be the sort that is compensatable in law. This harm is often of a physical nature as it is easier to prove, but psychological or financial harm, such as loss or damage to property, may also be compensatable. In addition, the harm must be reasonably foreseeable as a result of the duty of care being breached.

For example, if a nurse assesses and records that a patient has a high risk of developing pressure ulcers and does not implement actions to prevent them it is probable that the patient will develop such ulcers. This failure to act is a breach of duty of care.

This example also illustrates the fourth component of negligence, i.e. causation (see *Figure 6.1*). The cause of the harm needs to be directly linked to the breach in the duty of care.

Consider the case of a seriously ill child who has meningitis. A doctor prescribes antibiotics but the dose he gives is 10 times the normal dose. The child becomes deaf. Was the doctor negligent, and was the harm caused because of the doctor's actions? It appears at first that this is a clear case of negligence as the doctor had a duty of care which he breached by giving an incorrect drug dose and the child suffered harm as a result. But was the deafness caused on balance of probabilities by the overdose of antibiotics? Meningitis is an infection that can result in deafness so it is not possible to conclude that it was the drug overdose alone that caused the harm, so negligence cannot be proven (*Kay v Ayrshire and Arran Health Board* [1987] in Dimond 2015).

Determining liability can thus be problematic, even more so in the case of post-traumatic stress where a relative suffers severe shock following the death of a close family member (*McLoughlin v O'Brien* [1982] in Dimond, 2015). A statutory right for compensation for bereavement where a death has occurred as a result of negligence now exists, although grief itself is not a ground for a claim. There has been a range of other cases brought before the courts by both relatives and employees with respect to claiming compensation for post-traumatic stress syndrome.

Sometimes the claimant does not know that any harm has been caused until many years after an event, such as in cases of asbestosis. Now the claimant has 3 years from the realisation of harm to sue for negligence. For example, a female patient has a sterilisation as a means of contraception and is told it will be impossible to conceive. She becomes pregnant several years later and it is at that time she realises the harm and can begin a claim for negligence.

One exception to the rule that the harm caused must be reasonably foreseeable is known as the 'thin skull rule'. Occasionally a claimant has a weakness that was unknown both to himself and the defendant. As a result of the negligent act the claimant suffers harm that would not have occurred in most other patients. The defendant is therefore responsible and liable for this harm.

The case of *Smith v Leech Brain and Co Ltd* [1961] is the precedence case here where an employee suffered a burnt lip by a splash of molten metal. Although the burn was treated it later ulcerated and cancer of the lip was diagnosed. This spread throughout his body and he died as a result. The court held that the amount of damage suffered as a result of the initial burnt lip 'depended on the characteristics and constitution of the victim'. The defendant was responsible for all harm caused: the initial burnt lip, the foreseeable cancer of the lip, consequential secondary cancer and death (Wheeler, 2012).

You may think that more than one person was negligent in some of the following scenarios; identify them and explain how they could also have been negligent.

Activity

- Read the scenarios presented below, which are based on real negligence cases, to test your understanding. Use the four components that have to be proved by the claimant and decide for each:
- Who was negligent?
- How was their duty of care breached? Were the defendant's actions reasonable?
- What harm was caused? Was it foreseeable?
- Was causation directly a result of the breach of duty of care?

Scenario 1

In the cases *Wilsher v Essex Health Authority* [1986] and *Wilsher v Essex AHA* [1988] (McHale and Fox, 2007; Griffith and Tengnah, 2014; Dimond, 2015) a premature baby required oxygen therapy in the neonatal unit. This needed careful and continuous monitoring of oxygen concentrations in the baby's blood via a probe inserted into a blood vessel. A junior doctor inserted the probe into a vein instead of an artery. A senior doctor also made the same mistake. As a result, inaccurate oxygen levels were recorded. Because of this the baby was given too much oxygen by a nurse and suffered permanent damage to the retina of the eye and blindness.

- All three practitioners owed a duty of care to the baby and the baby did suffer harm.
- The nurse did not breach her duty of care because she administered oxygen based on the blood levels and could not have known that the doctors had incorrectly positioned the probe. Neither could the nurse be expected to recognise developing retinal damage as this was beyond her role and ability. She acted in a reasonable way.
- The junior doctor did not breach his duty of care because, although he inserted the probe incorrectly, he had asked his superior to check it. The junior doctor's actions were reasonable in asking for confirmation. The Bolam test applied.
- The senior doctor was found negligent because he breached his duty of care by failing to notice that the probe was in the wrong place. This resulted in harm to the baby which was foreseeable.

This case went to the House of Lords who held that the claimant had not proved that the excess oxygen had caused the blindness and they ordered a re-trial because of the issue of causation (Dimond, 2015).

Scenario 2

In the case of *Maynard v West Midlands Regional Health Authority* [1984] (Pattison, 2009; Griffith and Tengnah, 2014; Dimond, 2015) a patient presented at the hospital with symptoms of a chest complaint. The possible diagnosis included tuberculosis, Hodgkin's disease (a potentially fatal disease if not treated early enough), and two other conditions. The doctor decided to perform an invasive procedure and biopsy to help determine which condition the woman had rather than wait for sputum results which would confirm tuberculosis.

The procedure carried a risk of damage to a nerve affecting the vocal chords and the patient sued because this did indeed occur. The results of the sputum test later showed a diagnosis of tuberculosis.

In this case the doctor had a duty of care but there were different expert medical opinions as to whether this was breached. Some experts stated that they would have gone ahead with the biopsy without waiting for the sputum results because of the severity of one possible diagnosis. Others would have waited rather than expose the patient to a procedure which carried risks.

Eventually, after appeal to the House of Lords, the original decision of negligence was overturned based on equally acceptable differences of opinion, both of which were reasonable in the circumstances. The House of Lords held that:

> *in the medical profession there was room for differences of opinion and practice, and that the court's preference for one body of opinion over another was no basis for a conclusion of negligence*

and

> *It was not sufficient to establish negligence for the claimant [sic] to show that there was a body of competent opinion that considered the decision had been wrong if there was also a body of equally competent professional opinion that supported the decision as having been reasonable in the circumstances.*

Dimond 2015: 51

The burden of proof lay with the claimant who could not establish that the actions were unreasonable based on a balance of probabilities.

From these scenarios, you can see that there is much for the claimant to prove and opinions of other practitioners in the relevant field are sought to support the case. The question of what is reasonable is very important, along with the aspect of causation. Many cases first found on behalf of the claimant go to appeal or the House of Lords where the initial decision may be overturned. This is a very lengthy procedure, fraught with problems for the claimant who may choose to settle out of court.

It is important to emphasise that for the nurse, documentary evidence can play a crucial role in recalling events many years after the alleged negligence case has occurred.

Implications for the nurse

As students, practising under the supervision of a registered nurse, it should be almost impossible to be sued for negligence. However, if students knowingly collude with a registered nurse and do not follow recommended guidelines, policies and procedures, protocols and benchmarks they can find themselves answering a negligence claim in the civil court.

It is important that you keep up to date with current evidence and research and follow directives warning of specific known risks, which are made widely available in nursing literature, and know what the accepted standards of care are.

The Francis report (2013) called for a culture of openness and transparency which resulted in joint guidance from professional regulators including the NMC to recognise and take action if mistakes happen. This has led to the new duty of candour (Dix, 2015; NMC, 2015) being created. Three key points require the practitioner to tell the patient when something has gone wrong, to try to put it right and to apologise for the mistake. In many instances the patient is seeking this sort of explanation and apology rather than pursuing a claim for negligence. There are many other recommendations in the Francis report for both the individual practitioner and employing organisation to take heed of to enhance the quality of care.

You must ensure that your records are current, accurate and relevant. *Chapter 8* will look further at written communication.

Registered nurses should be aware of areas which have arisen in both professional discipline and negligence cases and be extra vigilant in these areas of practice.

References

Bolam v Friern Barnet HMC [1957] 2 All ER 118

Dimond B (2015) *Legal aspects of nursing*. 7th edn. Pearson Education, Harlow

Dix A (2015) Adhering to new duty of candour guidance. *Nursing Times* **111**(32/33): 17–19

Donoghue v Stevenson [1932] AC 562

Fletcher L, Buka P (2007) *A legal framework for caring*. 3rd edn. Macmillan, Basingstoke

Francis R (2013) Report of the Mid Staffordshire NHS Foundation Trust Public Inquiry http://webarchive.nationalarchives.gov.uk/20150407084003/http://www.midstaffs-publicinquiry.com/report

Griffith R, Tengnah C (2014) *Law and Professional Issues in Nursing*. 3rd edn. Sage, London

Kay v Ayrshire and Arran Health Board [1987] 2 All ER 417

Maynard v West Midlands Regional Health Authority [1984] 1 WLR 634

McHale J, Fox M (2007) *Health care law*. 2nd edn. Sweet and Maxwell, London

McLoughlin v O'Brien [1982] 2 all ER 298

Moody M (2001) Why nurses end up in court. *Nursing Times* **97**(8): 24–6

NHS England (2012) 6Cs. https://www.england.nhs.uk/wp-content/uploads/2012/12/6c-a5-leaflet.pdf (accessed 17 February 2016)

Nursing and Midwifery Council (2015) *The Code: Professional standards of practice and behaviour for nurses and midwives*. Nursing and Midwifery Council, London

Nursing and Midwifery Council (2016) Professional indemnity arrangement. www.nmc.org.uk/registration/staying-on-the-register/professional-indemnity-arrangement/ (accessed 17 February 2016)

Pattison D (2009) *Medical law and ethics*. 2nd edn. Sweet and Maxwell, London

Smith v Leech Brain & Co Ltd [1962] 2 QB 405, [1961] 3 All ER 1159

Wheeler N (2012) *Law, Ethics and Professional Issues for Nursing. A Reflective and Portfolio-Building Approach*. Routledge, London

Whitehouse v Jordan [1981] 1 All ER 267

Wilsher v Essex Health Authority [1986] 3 All ER 801

Wilsher v Essex AHA [1988] QB 730, CA

Section 3

This section is very broadly entitled 'communication' since nurses spend a lot of time communicating. This section also reflects a lot of the content of the Code (Nursing and Midwifery Council, 2015), which highlights vital communication skills.

Communication is performed in various different ways. Word of mouth, tone of voice, eye contact or not, sign and body language, facial expression and by electronic and written means. Each of these types of communication has legal, ethical and professional implications as the following two chapters demonstrate.

Documents issued by the Nursing and Midwifery Council will be cited which will inform on how to behave in practice and pitfalls to avoid. E.g. *The Code: Professional standards of practice and behaviour for nurses and midwives* (2015) and *Guidance on using social media responsibly* (2016).

Chapter 7 focuses on legal and ethical issues such as truthfulness/truth telling, choice, consent, confidentiality, autonomy and advocacy.

Chapter 8 looks at the many professional and practical aspects of written communication.

Activity

Make a list of the situations when you might be asked or required to disclose your own personal information.

Your list may include – visiting a dentist or doctor's surgery, giving personal details to a bank or building society, tax, benefits or housing issues, a child's school.

Specialist clinics or hospital departments may also want very intimate details so the best care and/or treatment can be offered in an accident and emergency department, outpatients department or specialised clinics for sexual or mental health issues.

Activity

- What type of environment would encourage you to disclose personal information?
- What specific characteristics would you like the listener to demonstrate?

You would probably prefer an environment that is quiet, private and comfortable and where you will not be overheard. You also may wish to have a chaperone of your choice.

You will want to be able to trust the listener and expect him/her to be relaxed and attentive, and be able explain things to you in a language you understand. You would perhaps question how this information will be used, what is going to happen as a consequence, and who will have access to this information. Most people would not wish to feel pressurised into revealing more than they wish. Other thoughts might include: what are 'they' going to do with this information?

Nursing and Midwifery Council (2015) *The Code: Professional standards of practice and behaviour for nurses and midwives.* Nursing and Midwifery Council, London

Nursing and Midwifery Council (2016) *Guidance on using social media responsibly.* Nursing and Midwifery Council, London

CHAPTER 7

Principles of communication in different contexts

Rights, responsibilities/duties

For many years there has been discussion over 'patients' rights'. Different patients' charters have been written by the Department of Health to indicate the standards patients can expect when receiving health care. Statutory legislation, such as the Human Rights Act 1998, has set out a series of rights anyone can expect in life. Rights are often used as a means for individuals to get their own way. However, for every 'right' a person has there is also a 'duty' or 'responsibility'.

See presentation: www.bihr.org.uk/my-human-rights

Cuthbert and Quallington (2008) discuss the links between these two complementary factors in an exploration of a rights-based approach to care. From a legal perspective Dimond (2008) highlights several areas where a patient has a legal right to:

- Health care (but not absolute)
- A reasonable standard of care
- Give consent
- Access health records
- Confidentiality
- Complain and have complaints dealt with speedily and effectively.

In addition, Thompson et al (2006) argue for the ethical right:

- to know
- to have privacy
- to treatment.

The King's Fund has produced a useful guide to the reforms and changes in health care provision and delivery following the implementation of the Health and Social Care Act 2013 see:

www.kingsfund.org.uk/topics/nhs-reform

Here is also a link to the government's outline and access to factsheets for the Care Act 2014 and the Carer's Rights Act 2014

www.gov.uk/government/publications/care-act-2014-part-1-factsheets

www.nhs.uk/conditions/social-care-and-support-guide/pages/carers-rights-care-act-2014.aspx

This discussion underpins the importance of communication in health care – there are so many facets to it.

To return to the list of patients' rights, not only do patients/clients have responsibilities and duties corresponding to their rights, but nurses also have responsibilities and duties towards their patients/clients and themselves.

Activity

Try to think of the duties/responsibilities a nurse has in response to patients' rights listed above.

Table 7.1 lists patients' rights and beside these the relevant standards required of nurses and midwives both for those who are students and those who are qualified, as stated in the Code (Nursing and Midwifery Council (NMC), 2015a).

In summary, this requires nurses – both students and qualified – to Prioritise People; Practise Effectively; Preserve Safety; Promote Professionalism and Trust.

Table 7.1. Patients' rights and nurses' duties/responsibilities	
Patients' rights	*Nurses' duties/responsibilities covered by the NMC (2015a) Code*
A right to healthcare	3. Make sure that people's physical, social and psychological needs are assessed and responded to
A right to care of a reasonable standard	2. Listen to people and respond to their preferences and concerns
	6. Always practise in line with the best available evidence
	13. Recognise and work within the limits of your competence
A right to consent	2. Listen to people and respond to their preferences and concerns
A right to confidentiality	5. Respect people's right to privacy and confidentiality
	25. Provide leadership to make sure people's wellbeing is protected and to improve their experience of the healthcare system

A right to complain	4. Act in the best interests of the patient at all times
	24. Respond to any complaints made against you professionally
	23. Cooperate with all investigations and audits
A (legal) right to know	7. Communicate clearly
	9. Share your skills, knowledge and experiences for the benefit of the people receiving care and your colleagues
	11. Be accountable for your decisions to delegate tasks and duties to other people
A right to dignity and privacy	1. Treat people as individuals and uphold their dignity
	16. Act without delay if you believe there is a risk to patient safety or public protection
A right to treatment	14. Be open and candid with all service users about all aspects of care and treatment, including when any mistakes or harm have taken place
	8. Work cooperatively
A right to not be discriminated against	17. Raise concerns immediately if you believe a person is vulnerable or at risk and needs extra support and protection
	19. Be aware of, and reduce as far as possible, any potential for harm associated with your practice
	15. Always offer help if an emergency arises in your practice setting or anywhere else
These are statements which apply overall to all the standards	12. Have in place an indemnity arrangement which provides appropriate cover for any practice you take on as a nurse or midwife in the United Kingdom
	21. Uphold your position as a registered nurse or midwife
	22. Fulfil all registration requirements

Table 7.1 may make it seem as if the nurse has no rights, but nurses do have rights. For example, if a nurse has suffered harm as a consequence of violence, he or she can take action. According to Dimond (2008, 2015) a nurse can:

- Sue the aggressor personally for trespass to the person
- Sue the employer if the nurse can establish that there has been a breach of the employer's duty of care to them

- Obtain compensation from the criminal courts following the successful prosecution of the assailant

Activity

Access the National Audit Office and government websites and view the incidence of reported violence towards NHS staff.
www.nao.org.uk/report/a-safer-place-to-work-protecting-nhs-hospital-and-ambulance-staff-from-violence-and-aggression/
http://webarchive.nationalarchives.gov.uk/+/www.dh.gov.uk/en/mediacentre/pressreleases/dh_124684

- Claim compensation from the Criminal Injuries Compensation Authority
- Possibly receive statutory sick pay and social benefits if eligible.

The Health and Safety Executive publishes guidance about violence-related harm on its website: www.hse.gov.uk/violence/information.htm. Hopefully this will not be needed by you, but you may be able to help a colleague.

Additional points need to be mentioned regarding the patient's response:

- Having rights does not mean you are bound to use them
- Having rights does not mean that their exercise in unlimited
- There are positive rights and negative rights with negative rights being, in general, stronger than positive ones. That means the right to refuse treatment. If a treatment is subsequently given against the patient's will, it is technically criminal assault.

Here is a link to the Department of Health's guidelines to patients and how their wishes are honoured: www.nhs.uk/chq/pages/899.aspx?categoryid=68

This all leads the discussion to the key right of 'consent'.

Consent

Consent incorporates legal, ethical and professional issues and there is extensive written and electronic literature to guide practitioners and patients, although it is fully acknowledged that nurses are not the sole custodians of consent. Field-specific variations mean that alternative methods of handling the differences may be needed.

During an assessment interview with a patient on admission you start to determine what the patient expects from his/her time in your care. You may determine how anxious the patient is, how much, if anything, he/she wants to know about what is wrong with him/her and how ready the patient is to discuss the implications of the disease process. All of this has implications for the nurse when he/she asks a patient for consent for a nursing procedure.

Activity

Access these links and identify how consent may be given noting three key features that are crucial in gaining valid consent:
www.nhs.uk/chq/pages/899.aspx?categoryid=68
http://rcnhca.org.uk/sample-page/confidentiality-and-consent/consent/

Gillon (1985) states that after all the input, the person will accept rather than reject what is offered. Brykczyńska (1989), on the other hand, talks of alternatives and the patient taking the initiative to empower those who will provide the treatment/care.

There will be some people who, if they were the patient, would want to find out all about the treatment/care on offer but ultimately would trust the health-care professionals to do the best for them. Others would want to know about the choices on offer, and would want to make their own choice. Another group would rather not know about what could go wrong or know the finer details of the proposed care and would prefer to trust the health-care professionals. It is the trust the patient places with the health-care professionals that forms the basis of consent; i.e. the person must already trust you in order to give consent (Cuthbert and Quallington, 2008). Having assessed the amount of information the patient wants to hear the nurse must clearly record this in the nursing records along with a patient's request for only limited information if that is his/her wish. Factors that could hinder the understanding of information could include hearing impediments, the disease process itself, distractions or difficulty in understanding English.

Activity

Explore further the issue of capacity and what is required if a patient lacks capacity via this link: www.nhs.uk/conditions/consent-to-treatment/pages/introduction.aspx

Why is consent needed?

If a nurse approaches a patient and, without any positive indication on the part of the patient, carries out a procedure (however well intentioned) then the patient has the right to pursue legal action (Dimond, 2008; Pattison, 2009).

This could be trespass, which could lead to:

- A civil or criminal action for battery – if touched without permission
- A civil action for assault – fear of being touched.

The information threshold for battery is, however, very low (Pattison, 2009). To succeed in trespass, it has to be proven that there had been a real lack of consent by the patient, as demonstrated in the case *Chatterton v Gerson* [1981].

However, no battery is committed where the patient understands the broad nature of the treatment, even if this understanding is arrived at from accessing sources of information other than the nurse or other health-care professional seeking consent. However, if a nurse or health-care professional fails to explore the risks and implications of the treatment being proposed then the claim would be for negligence, not battery (Pattison, 2009). A patient can only take an action for battery if:

- He/she is treated against his/her will (assuming the patient has the capacity to give consent)
- The patient receives a different treatment from the one he or she originally consented to
- The consent was obtained by means of fraud.

The role of the nurse has advanced greatly, with many nurses making autonomous decisions about the diagnosis and subsequent treatment/care options for patients (such as the nurse performing an endoscope procedure for a patient); hence the nurse is required to understand the legislation related to consent when undertaking nurse-led procedures.

There are times when consent would not be required.

- *Life-threatening emergency*: This could be if a person has a cardiac arrest. Unless the patient had expressly stated that he or she did not want cardiopulmonary resuscitation (CPR) then it would be expected that CPR would be carried out if considered medically appropriate.

- *When a patient is sectioned under a relevant section of the Mental Health Act (1983 amended 2007)*: In this case medication can be given without consent. See later discussions.
- *Where public health is at risk under the Public Health (Control of Disease) Act 1984*: A patient may need to be isolated in a single room in hospital because of an infectious disease. Consent would be requested but could be overridden for the health needs of the majority.

Who can give consent?

Adults

No adult can give consent on behalf of another adult if the latter is legally competent and has the capacity to make his or her own informed choice. The Mental Capacity Act 2005 does make provision for the appointment of a lasting power of attorney, and this individual can give consent on behalf of another (Dimond, 2008). However, where no lasting power of attorney has been appointed by the patient there may be situations when the carers/relatives/ friends are asked for their suggestions as to how the individual would normally react, but they cannot sign the consent form; consent needs to be given by the person concerned. A person, unless otherwise assessed, is considered to be mentally competent under Section 1(2) of the Mental Capacity Act 2005; the criteria to be used in assessing competence are set by Sections 2 and 3 of the Act (Dimond, 2008).

Activity

Access the Mental Capacity Act 2005 at www.legislation.gov.uk/ukpga/2005/9/ contents It would be beneficial for you to familiarise yourself with this piece of legislation. In particular, read Section 4 which refers to 'Best Interests'.

Vulnerable patients

Included in this category are some elderly, mentally incapacitated or mentally ill people. A number of people may be mentally incapacitated for a short time as a result of sedation or unconsciousness.

There are many people who fall into this category of vulnerable adult. Overall, the principle that must be applied is that the best interests of the patient must be paramount. 'Best interests' goes wider than best medical interests and should include factors such as the individuality and wishes of the patient when he/she was competent (e.g. advance directive), his/her current wishes, his/her general wellbeing, and his/her spiritual and religious welfare. According to Joyce (2007) 'best interest' does not reflect the personal views of the decision-maker, instead it requires an objective view on both the current and future interests of the person.

Trying to provide care in the best interests of the patient is not always easy. For example, relatives of older people, although they cannot formally give consent to treatment (unless they have a lasting power of attorney under the Mental Capacity Act 2005), can influence the care that is given. However, this may not always reflect the patient's wishes at that time. This could be because many older people are tired of living. When younger the patient may have undergone treatment to stay alive, but now he/she is ready to die. This does not imply that the person would want to end his/her life, just that he/she would not wish to prolong it. In this instance, non-intervention would be the patient's choice if he/she was able to give his/her consent.

With patients who are mentally incapacitated from any cause, the relatives, carers and friends may be able to give an indication of their wishes. The nurse should know which local policies to follow for guidance on vulnerable patients. The *Deprivation of Liberty Safeguards* (Department of Health, 2007) came into effect in 2009 to safeguard those whose decision-making ability was incapacitated to ensure that their human rights are considered. In order to deprive an incapacitated patient of his or her liberty two health and social care professionals (including a mental health nurse) must assess the patient to ensure the proposed liberty deprivation is in the best interest of the patient. The patient can be detained for up to 12 months; however, a review can be authorised earlier, and the patient is appointed an advocate. An assessment is also made to determine whether the patient would be better protected under a compulsory detention under the Mental Health Act 1983 (amended 2007).

The basis for valid consent is that it must be voluntary, informed, cover the act performed and be from a legally competent source.

When dealing with mental health patients, all the factors listed above apply, but there are other legal aspects a nurse must consider relating to the Mental Health Act 1983, the Mental Capacity Act 2005, and the Safeguarding Vulnerable Groups Act 2006 (which also encompasses the safeguarding of children in specific circumstances).

The Mental Health Act 1983 (amended 2007) identifies two groups of patients:

- Voluntary patients, i.e. those who have asked for treatment and are sometimes called 'informal' patients
- Detained or sectioned patients who have complex mental health problems, may have no insight into their condition, and who are 'detained' for their own or the public's safety.

Following the Bournewood case (*R v Bournewood Community and Mental Health NHS Trust*, see Department of Health, 1999) there is now another group recognised by the House of Lords. This consists of patients who are incapable of giving consent to admission to hospital and have not been detained under the Mental Health Act 1983. Staff have a duty of care to act in the patient's best interests under common law powers. However, even in the more recent legislation there is no clear legal definition under the Mental Capacity Act 2005 of 'best interest' (Joyce, 2007; Dimond, 2015). However, the Act does have a list of factors that must be checked for the assessment of a person's capacity. If a patient is assessed under the Mental Capacity Act 2005 to lack the capacity to give valid consent, and if he/she does not have a lasting power of attorney appointed, the patient will be allocated an Independent Mental Capacity Advocate to represent his/her wishes.

The Mental Health Act 1983 was amended in 2007 to introduce the Independent Mental Health Advocacy Service. As with the Independent Mental Capacity Advocate, this advocate will work with the interest of the patient accessing mental health care. Consent should always be sought from mentally ill patients but there are some differences. Voluntary or informal patients can refuse to have treatment when asked for consent. This refusal must be respected unless there has been such a deterioration in the patient's condition that he/she then falls into the second category and has to be detained under an appropriate section of the Mental Health Act 1983. Common law powers to treat in the patient's best interests must be observed. The civil detention provisions under Part 2 of the Mental Health Act 1983, as amended, states there are legal requirements of mental health-care providers when dealing with consent issues. Individuals who are detained under the Mental Health Act 1983 may be prescribed medication for their mental health condition. However, it is important that the nurse is familiar with sections 57, 58 and 59 to determine the particular legal definition of 'treatment'; these sections of the Act will also establish under which circumstances medication and electroconvulsive therapy (ECT) can be given to a patient sectioned under the Act. Correct forms and strict records must be kept of the patient's detention status and ability to consent.

Activity

Read: Mughal AF (2014) Understanding and using the Mental Capacity Act. Nursing Times 110(21): 16–18
Identify the key principles and how the Act may be used

Minors

A parent, or someone to whom parental responsibility has been given, can give consent for treatment to a child. The law specifies the definition of consent and its boundaries.

According to the Family Law Reform Act 1969, for medical, surgical and dental purposes a child can give consent to treatment when aged 16 years. A later Act of Parliament, the Children Act 1989 (as amended 2004) states that the wishes and feelings of the child should be ascertained and considered in the light of his or her age and understanding. This is obviously going to vary according to the child's mental age and experience.

It was established in *Gillick v West Norfolk and Wisbech AHA* [1986] that a child under the age of 16 years can legally have the capacity to give consent to a medical examination and treatment (including contraceptive treatment) providing the child could demonstrate sufficient maturity and intelligence to understand the implications of what was consented to. The Gillick principle reflects the young person's transition from a child to adulthood. However, nurses need to be aware that under the Sexual Offences Act 2003, it is a criminal offence to procure sexual intercourse with a child under the age of 16 years. Thus, contraceptive treatment and advice should only be given on clinical grounds. Lord Fraser, in the Gillick case, issued guidelines (the Fraser Guidelines) to protect nurses from being accused of breaching the Sexual Offences Act 2003; these guidelines have been extended in section 13 of the Sexual Offences Act. This may mean not telling the child's parent(s) about the treatment if it is in the interest of the child's welfare not to do so.

Activity

Locate a copy of the Fraser Guidelines and read them.

Summary

This section has provided a brief overview of some pertinent legislation related to the concept of consent. However, you are advised to read around the subject areas in greater depth in order to develop a more comprehensive understanding of what constitutes valid consent.

You may have noticed that there is no law specifically on consent, but the issues arise from other areas of law.

A summary of the laws involved is shown in *Table 7.2.*

Table 7.2. Summary of laws involved in consent	
Field	*Legal source*
General principles	Trespass, assault, battery, negligence, common law principles
Mental health	Mental Health Act, Mental Capacity Act Safeguarding Vulnerable Groups Act
Child	Family Reform Act, Children Act
Learning disabilities	Children Act (if under 16 years), Mental Health Act, Mental Capacity Act, Safeguarding Vulnerable Groups Act

Here are three further sources regarding different facets of consent:

- Charnock E, Owens D (2013) *Patient Consent: Nursing & Health Survival Guide*. Routledge, Oxon
- Royal College of Nursing (2015) http://rcnhca.org.uk/sample-page/ confidentiality-and-consent/consent/
- NHS Choices (2014) http://www.nhs.uk/conditions/consent-to-treatment/ pages/introduction.aspx

Ethical and professional issues of consent

Activity

Look back to *Section 1* and check the name of the authors who outlined the five ethical principles. Now consider how these ethical principles relate to this section.

All patients, including those from any of the groups discussed above, need to have information about the choices they have to make. The choice may be to accept one or other option or refuse the treatment on offer. For the patient to be able to do this the information needs to be given truthfully but in a way that enables understanding, and at a rate that is acceptable to the individual. That is why the importance of individual assessment was highlighted at the beginning of this section. If the patient is to have autonomy, the choice that is given must not be one of 'take it or leave it' or 'Hobson's choice'. There needs to be a genuine choice and, as stated earlier, the consequences of each option need to be given.

The nurse's duty of care includes the duty to inform – see details on the Bolam Test with regards to negligence in Chapter 6.

This means that any breach is actionable, but only if harm can be proved. This contrasts with trespass, where harm does not have to be proved.

Truth-telling/truthfulness

From the activity on page 67 you should have been able to identify Thiroux and Krasemann (2007) as the authors of the principle of truth-telling (and of autonomy). Telling the truth is a value which is usually encouraged in early childhood. Thiroux and Krasemann (2007) endorse this, saying it is one of the hallmarks of true communication.

In 1999, Rumbold suggested the following activity; it is still useful.

Activity

Ask yourself whether you agree or disagree with the following statements:
- To tell the truth is right.
- One should tell the truth on all occasions.
- There are occasions when to tell a lie is justified.

You probably said that you agree with the first statement, but that you could argue for and against the other two.

The truth comes in many forms and sometimes the truth may not be suitable as it is too blunt and sounds uncaring. Does that mean a lie has to be told, or will you be 'economical' with the truth?

Think of some of the problems which could follow a lie. You will have to remember what you said for a start and then tell everyone else what you have said so that they can maintain the story. At a later date if you are somehow confronted with the lie, you may lose all trust and credibility.

Economy with the truth can also pose problems. You could easily be confronted with the fuller version of the truth and have to explain your actions, even if this may have been done to minimise harm (non-maleficence) to the patient. Whichever route you take there will be pitfalls.

By being sensitive to a patient's needs, there may be rare occasions when a person's condition might lead you to be selective (although never untruthful) about the information you give. How can a nurse tell the truth about a procedure? Consider this scenario:

Nurse: Hello Mr Grant, I've come with your suppositories.
Mr Grant: What are they for?
Nurse: You said you were very constipated. They help the bowel to work.
Mr Grant: How are you going to put them in?
Nurse: If you get on to your bed, turn on to your left side with your bottom near to the edge, then I will insert them having lubricated them first.
Mr Grant: Will it hurt?
Nurse: It may feel a little uncomfortable, so you need to try to relax.
Mr Grant: How quick do they work?
Nurse: You'll get some sensation to want to have your bowels open quite quickly, but you need to try to hold on for about 20 minutes for them to work properly.

On the face of it there is nothing wrong with the exchange between the nurse and Mr Grant, however:

- Did he have a choice?
- Was a choice necessary?
- Did the nurse outline any other consequences apart from success?

The possible need for immediate access to a toilet was not mentioned and the controversial 'truth' that 'if I insert these badly I could actually rupture your rectum' was not mentioned either.

What would you consider to be adequate as consent to this procedure?

This example may seem simple, but it does illustrate some of the points previously mentioned. Sometimes nurses have to face up to problems of truth-telling which are not of their making. The one which is often quoted is that of discussing diagnosis or prognosis with relatives without the patient's knowledge or vice versa.

An area where telling the truth can be difficult is if a patient refuses vital medication. There has been a lot of debate over this issue and court cases have followed when patients have been given medication in a disguised form. The NMC (2015b) has issued standards if a patient is unable to give informed consent and the medication is in their best interests. Disguised medication must never be used for the health-care team's convenience. In effect, the nurses are not telling the truth in their actions, but this may be seen as ethically the best course of action as the principle of least harm is being applied.

Truth-telling is only the first part of the process of giving information; after information has been given, then the patient has to make a choice. This is where autonomy comes in.

Autonomy

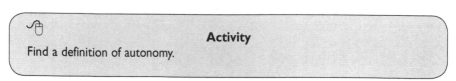

Activity

Find a definition of autonomy.

People have their individual differences, they have their own ways of being moral, and, as much as is possible, they follow the dictates of their own intelligence and conscience (Thiroux and Krasemann, 2007). To do this they have to have an opportunity to choose. They also need sufficient information to make the choice (Fletcher and Buka, 2007). The options put before patients should be in their best interests, and also set in the context of the 'common good' of the patients in that part of the wider health service (Thompson et al, 2006).

When people in the health-care setting have a choice they tend to follow one of four routes when confronted with needing to give consent to a procedure:

- The patient can agree with the nurse and submit to the procedure
- The patient may ask a lot of questions which the nurse must answer truthfully or, equally truthfully, acknowledge their limitations (NMC, 2015a) before a decision can be made
- The patient may first agree to the procedure and then later refuse
- The patient can refuse to have the procedure (for a variety of reasons).

These are four ways of expressing personal freedom or autonomy.

At the beginning of *Chapter 7* we looked at two definitions of consent. Gillon (1985) assumed that, 'the patient would accept rather than reject some course of action that will affect him or her'. This is the assumption most of us (if we are truly honest) would make when asking for a patient's consent. How do we handle the situation when a person refuses outright, as in the medication example above? The easy answer would be to record 'drug refused' on the medication record.

Activity

What else needs to be considered when a patient is making a decision about consent?

The temptation, when patients refuse something that is offered and considered to be the best course of action, is to try to persuade them to change their mind (see Thompson et al, 2006). This is sometimes described as 'paternalism' — the idea that we know best, so you must follow our instructions (Melia, 2004). This does not allow for the patient's individual freedom. Having argued this, some people may say that to have a choice is very confusing, and that in fact health-care professionals do know best (Tingle and Cribb, 2007). It is one thing to stand in a supermarket and try to decide which brand of baked beans to buy but quite another to make a decision about surgery or drug therapy.

In the authors' experience, patients receiving verbal and non-verbal messages from staff can be subject to the following:

• Intense pressure to conform
• Remarks which indicate the staff's displeasure
• Ostracism
• Reduced levels of care.

Unfortunately, sometimes staff do not know how to deal with the situation of rejection, they take it personally and respond accordingly. But if we believe it is a person's right to choose then we have to accept the person's right to refuse as well. The care we give to that individual may change to accommodate the different care required, but the standard must be as high (NMC, 2015a).

Autonomy is not always possible. Many people do not have the capacity to choose. It is very important to create opportunities for autonomy and also to respect the autonomy an individual is capable of. Clearly, an infant, an unconscious patient and some people with learning disabilities and mental health problems will not be able to make an autonomous choice (Rumbold, 1999).

When it is necessary to create autonomy, in certain circumstances this can be done by gently putting the situation back into patients' hands and giving them time to think about their decision. Often nurses are in such a hurry that there is little time for patients to deliberate and so they make the choice they think the nurse would like. Not everybody behaves in this way. There may be occasions when you might see your colleagues behaving in a less than helpful way towards patients who are exercising their autonomy. Such a situation might require you to undertake an additional role – that of advocate.

Advocacy

An advocate is one who pleads on behalf of another. Advocacy is about power: influencing those who have power for those who do not, particularly where a person lacks the capacity to make decisions (Dimond, 2008, 2015).

Activity

In your everyday life, when might you act as an advocate for another?

Your answer may include speaking to a teacher on behalf of your child, acting as a go-between for friends who have quarrelled or signing a petition for or against something.

Advocacy is also a role that is used in the courts and that is why it is sometimes considered to be 'high powered'. It is a role that can be used effectively in the clinical setting to speak on behalf of one or a group of patients.

It must always be remembered that advocates plead for another person and express his or her wishes, not their own.

Activity

Think of situations when you have been or might have to be an advocate for a patient.

The situation in which you may act as advocate will differ according to your area of nursing practice, but there will be similar themes.
• The patient is unable or unwilling to speak on behalf of him or herself

- You have been one of a group who has campaigned for change, such as a change of time for a procedure
- You defend a patient's decision by speaking to a colleague to explain it.

There will be some areas of advocacy which are relatively simple. The examples below follow no particular order:

- A patient does not know/understand information. This may be after a doctor has spoken to a patient about a procedure. Afterwards the patient asks you what it all meant. You are advised to recall the doctor to answer the patient's questions in a manner the patient can understand. Nurses may only answer questions within their level of knowledge (NMC, 2015a), otherwise they may be judged in a court of law if a complaint of negligence is made (see *Chapter 6*).
- A patient is incapable of making a decision
- A patient cannot complete the daily menu sheet and you do it after discussion
- An adult patient is asleep and has requested that he should not be disturbed; it is therefore not appropriate for a visitor to see the patient. The nurse acts as advocate for the patient when asking the visitor to return later. It is a request that may not be acceptable and the patient cannot ask for him or herself.
- Another example could be where a qualified children's nurse in the accident and emergency department discovers that the drug dose prescribed for a 3-year-old is twice what it should be. Ethically it would not be in the child's best interest for the nurse to administer the drug, nor would it value the child's life. Professionally the nurse is accountable for her actions and would have to justify why she would give the large dose if she took that course of action. Legally the nurse could be sued for negligence if harm occurred to the child as a result of the drug overdose. To act as this child's advocate, the nurse needs to return the prescription sheet to the medical officer and ask for the dose to be checked and amended.

Other more complex areas of advocacy can be seen in *Figure 7.1*. These are all areas where a nurse may get involved. Each of these areas will now be discussed, looking at the legal, ethical and professional implications for each.

Figure 7.1. Areas of advocacy.

Patient incapable of making a decision

This area of advocacy has been discussed under the section on consent. In all cases the best interests of the patient should be paramount.

Patient or visitor complaints

If a complaint is voiced, you should listen and not comment or act defensively. All NHS trusts have to have a policy for complaints (under the Hospital Complaints Procedure Act 1985, superseded by the National Health Service [Complaints] Amendment Regulations 2006, SI 2006 no. 2084; Dimond, 2008) and the nurse acts as advocate by advising the complainant of the procedure to follow. Sometimes you may have to follow the complaint further if there is need for a report. You would then have to investigate or answer questions to establish whether there was cause for complaint. The outcome may be that you find yourself campaigning on behalf of the patient or relative, because you discover that there is a sound ethical reason for doing so, for example, it is the beneficent thing to do. The Patient Liaison Advocacy Service (PALS) has been part of the NHS since 2002, when it was launched by the Department of Health as part of the NHS Plan (Department of Health, 2002); PALS is a service that helps to provide relevant information for patients, and to support members of staff in their endeavour to help patients.

Patient abuse

Patient abuse can result in whistle-blowing if a member of staff is seen to be abusing a patient and misusing the privileged relationship a nurse has (NMC, 2015). The Public Interest Disclosure Act 1998 gives protection to the whistle-blower as long as correct procedures have been followed (NMC, 2015). However, all staff should follow their own employers' policy related to safeguarding patients and raising concerns. As mentioned in chapter 2 the Care Quality Commission have also issued regulations related to raising concerns about standards of care to protect patients from abuse; additionally, NHS England (2016) have published *Freedom to speak up: the raising concerns (whistleblowing) policy for NHS* to provide clear information to health-care providers about their responsibilities related to safeguarding patients.

Alternatively, you may see a relative abusing a patient and have to act as an advocate in a difficult situation. Again, it is important to remember that you are pleading on behalf of someone else and with his or her wishes.

Specific needs of vulnerable patient groups

The elderly, children, and those with learning disabilities and mental health problems are vulnerable in different ways. One common denominator is that they are often without power to deal with situations. Sometimes there will be group advocates who may have nothing to do with any health-care professional. These include, for example, NSPCC and Age UK. These organisations work on behalf of such patient groups on common problems although individual needs are also dealt with.

Relatives need help following a death

This situation will obviously depend on where you work. Many relatives need someone to act as an advocate when there has been a death. They may need someone to telephone to find out information which they cannot do in their state of grief.

Other relatives may find themselves in the position of making a decision about the harvesting of a loved one's organs to donate to another person. At this time, they need someone to act as a go-between so that they understand the process and do not feel too pressurised.

This may all sound very positive and a role which nurses would find satisfying. Unfortunately, this is not always so.

Problems of advocacy

There are various problems with advocacy (Melia, 2004). It can:

- Cause disrupted relationships between colleagues from different disciplines
- Lead a nurse to champion one patient but not another, leading to injustice
- Be very time-consuming and therefore unpopular with the advocate, while also making the advocate unpopular as he or she may not be able to take an equal load of the work in a team
- Cause conflict between the nurse's professional role and the interests or wishes of the patient.

Additional legislation and advocacy

Human Rights Act 1998

There are a number of rights that human beings should have which are the founding principles of the Human Rights Act. These are listed by Dimond (2008) in an appendix where she also outlines the continuing effects of this law.

A useful pictorial version of aspects of the Human Rights Act can be accessed at www.humanrights.com/what-are-human-rights/international-human-rights-law.html You may notice that there are a different number of human rights listed than from the Geneva Convention (1945). It is interesting to web-search the history of this subject. Maybe explore www.humanrights.com or any of the many information websites. This may help with your reasoning as to why so many laws have been developed with highly ethical content, to protect all groups of people in society.

Public Interest Disclosure Act 1998

This act has been introduced to protect those who, for whatever reason, have cause to 'whistle blow' in an organisation, provided they follow set protocols. This is obviously a great step forward from ostracism, dismissal and other negative responses individuals have encountered in the past when acting as an advocate.

Table 7.3 includes questions and actions an advocate may need to consider and their outcomes. This table demonstrates the legal, ethical and professional issues related to advocacy.

Table 7.3. Advocacy: Questions, actions and likely outcomes	
Questions	
1. Is it legal?	• Yes, OK proceed • No, e.g. dying patient wants overdose of drugs – cannot proceed
2. Is it ethical?	• Yes, OK proceed • No, e.g. relatives want you to be dishonest on their behalf – cannot proceed
3. Is it professional?	• Yes, OK proceed • No, e.g. patient wants to give you a bribe for preferential treatment – cannot proceed
4. What help is required?	

Actions	*Outcome*
Simple advocacy: No risk to advocate • education • explanation • encouragement • empowerment	Individual acts for him or herself
Intermediate advocacy: Some risk to advocate • speak to another on behalf of an individual • speak to another on behalf of a group • suggest alternatives • suspend action	Advocate acts for individual who may then act for him/herself
Complicated advocacy: High risk to advocate • communicate widely: – whistle to blow? • challenge system • change practice • count cost – physical, emotional, professional	There may be some results of the action but this is often at personal cost

References

Brykczyńska G, ed (1989) *Ethics in paediatric nursing*. Chapman and Hall, London

Chatterton v Gerson [1981] 1AII ER 257

Cuthbert S, Quallington J (2008) *Values for care practice*. Reflect Press Ltd, Exeter

Department of Health (1999) *Health Service Circular HSC 1998/122 L v Bournewood Community and Mental Health NHS Trust Decision by the House of Lords in the Appeal*. Department of Health, London

Department of Health (2002) *The NHS Plan*. The Stationery Office, London

Department of Health (2007) *Deprivation of liberty safeguards and Mental Capacity Act 2005 local implementation networks*. The Stationery Office, London

Dimond B (2008) *Legal aspects of nursing*. 5th edn. Pearson Education, Harlow

Dimond B (2015) *Legal aspects of nursing*. 7th edn. Pearson Education, Harlow

Fletcher L, Buka P (2007) *A legal framework for caring*. 3rd edn. Macmillan, Basingstoke

Gillick v West Norfolk and Wisbech AHA [1986] AC 112 (HL)

Gillon R (1985) *Philosophical medical ethics*. John Wiley, London

Joyce T (2007) *Best interests: Guidance on determining the best interests of adults who lack the capacity to make a decision (or decisions) for themselves [England and Wales]*. British Psychological Society, Leicester

Melia K (2004) *Health care ethics*. Sage Publications, London

Mughal AF (2014) Understanding and using the Mental Capacity Act. *Nursing Times* **110**(21): 16–18

NHS England (2016) *Freedom to speak up: the raising concerns (whistleblowing) policy for NHS*. NHS England, London

Nursing and Midwifery Council (2015a) *The Code: Professional standards of practice and behaviour for nurses and midwives*. Nursing and Midwifery Council, London

Nursing and Midwifery Council (2015b) *Standards for medicines management*. Nursing and Midwifery Council, London

Pattison D (2009) *Medical law and ethics*. 2nd edn. Sweet and Maxwell, London

Rumbold G (1999) *Ethics in nursing practice*. 3rd edn. Baillière Tindall, Edinburgh

Thiroux JP, Krasemann KW (2007) *Ethics: Theory and practice* 9th edn. Prentice Hall, New Jersey

Thompson IE, Melia KM, Boyd KM (2006) *Nursing ethics*. 5th edn. Churchill Livingstone, Edinburgh

Tingle J, Cribb A, eds (2007) *Nursing law and ethics* 3rd edn. Blackwell Science, Oxford

CHAPTER 8

Written communication

The final chapter of this book looks at the vital aspect of written communication. The way information is communicated in a written format has changed considerably over the last few years and in many circumstances neither paper nor pen is used. However, the whole issue of record keeping is still a crucial component of nursing practice. Within the Code (Nursing and Midwifery Council (NMC), 2015) the word 'communication' or something similar is mentioned many times in the 16 pages of script! This would indicate that it is vitally important. Not all of the references are related to written communication, but what happens needs to be recorded in an appropriate manner within your own sphere of practice. Communication is not just a 'paper exercise'.

 There are numerous legal, ethical and professional issues surrounding written communication. The professional aspects are considered first. These include the types of written material and their importance and the role of the nurse in dealing with written records. Some of the laws that have influenced the professional guidelines are identified and legal implications for practice are outlined. Finally, a variety of ethical issues relating to records and record keeping are discussed as they affect the role of the student and the qualified nurse.

Activity

- Make a list of all the different documents that you have to consult or complete in your area of clinical practice. Compare and contrast how this may be different from other clinical areas you have worked in.
- What do you consider are the pros and cons of the different types of documents you have to deal with?
- Clinical records are a vital part of care. Are your records electronic or paper? What are the advantages and disadvantages of each?
- In 1987, Siegler gave an example of a patient who asked how many people would read his documents – he was told 75. However, records are primarily written for professional staff caring for the individual and this includes the patient themselves.
- Read the Code (NMC, 2015) and make a note of each of the other statements you think link to communication.
- Find a definition of confidentiality.

Professional aspects of documentation

The NMC (2015) highlights very clearly in many sections of the Code the importance of the communication that happens when dealing with patients, clients and colleagues. Nurses and midwives are now rarely involved in handwritten communication of record keeping as electronic record keeping and openness in communication is now in process. Computer literacy is also vital in order to input patient information accurately.

Some records (see *Table 8.1*) may be read by all of the people you have listed. In addition there are records that are held by the patient or parent which are brought to the professional when relevant. These include antenatal records, child immunisation records and privately funded records such as X-rays and second opinions.

Table 8.1. Examples of nursing records	
Care plans	• Assessment sheets • Plans for specific care • Handwritten/electronic core care plans • Daily summaries of care given and reactions to this • Evaluations of care given and subsequent assessments
Charts for	• Fluid balance • Weight • Mood • Neurological observations • Nutritional intake • Blood pressure • Wound assessment, etc.
Records used by the multidisciplinary team (MDT)	• Accident/incident forms • Discharge letters/referral letters, consent forms • Prescription charts • Do not actively resuscitate (DNAR) forms • Single assessment documentation

• Consider who might read this documentation – make a list – how does this influence what you write?

If records are needed for a court case related to any aspect of care, then all the personnel involved in that case would be entitled to read relevant parts of the patient's records. Owing to the fact people from different backgrounds will be reading the records, it is important that they are written in a format that will be understood by everyone. It is also much easier and safer to read a record that is in a logical and chronological order. It is vital that all records are completed correctly. See the information and the web link on the next page.

Here are some of the statements in the Code (NMC, 2015) mentioned earlier which are important in communication:

- 1.3 Avoid making assumptions and recognise diversity and individual choice
- 2.1 Work in partnership with people to make sure you deliver care effectively
- 2.4 Respect the level to which people receiving care want to be involved in decisions about their own health, wellbeing and care
- 2.5 Respect, support and document a person's right to accept of refuse care and treatment
- 3.3 Act in partnership with those receiving care, helping them to access relevant health and social care, information and support when they need it
- 5.1 Respect a person's right to privacy in all aspects of their care.
- 5.4 Share necessary information with other healthcare professionals and agencies only when the interests of patient safety and public protection override the need for confidentiality.

Completing client records

Making computerised or hand written paper records it is vital that:

- They are factual, objective, unbiased, consecutive, consistent and accurate
- They are completed as soon as possible after the event
- They are written in conjunction with the patient/carer and written so that the latter can understand the content
- It is obvious that the care has been planned on the basis of assessment, then implemented and subsequently evaluated
- They are clear and, if hand written, permanent and able to be photocopied
- They are accurately dated, timed and signed, with the name printed by the signature. A qualified nurse may have to sign all records created by a student nurse.
- They are unambiguous, with any alterations crossed through and signed
- Records should NOT include abbreviations, jargon, meaningless phrases, irrelevant speculation or derogatory, offensive or subjective statements.

Do refer to: www.gov.uk/government/publications/serious-crime-bill-computer-misuse – there are clauses whereby health-care staff can be called to account about anything related to serious crime and particularly when it involves computerised records and other data about patients in their care.

Points to consider:

- It is important to type records or complete forms as soon as possible after the event. It is impossible to remember precise details after time has elapsed and you may have done a variety of things in between, even if you know you have got to remember the details.
- Different words can have subtle different meanings which could convey different sets of circumstances. For example the words 'slipped' and 'fell' could both mean an individual was once upright and was then horizontal. The reasons behind this position could be something external – slipped on a spilt substance or internal – fell because of a change in blood pressure. The consequences if a court case ensued could be very different.
- If you are in an environment where there are paper records, all the different points related to record keeping apply. It is vital that these are legible for all the reasons mentioned above.
- With the increasing reliance on computer predictive recognition, beware that what is written is what you want to state, not only is confidentiality of password and safeguarding of access important but also the legal and ethical implications which will be looked at later in the chapter.
- When drug doses are administered via a bar code it is important to be aware that there can be 'mis-reads' of stock update and potentially the drug will not be administered. For all drug administration via whatever source, the drug required, its strength and the subsequent dose must all be checked – preferably by more than one person
- When making a computerised record ensure it is an honest record with the accurate date and time - lots of cases have been reported of no record of comments concerning complaints.
- Computers are only as good as the inputter!

Nursing is just one of the professions contributing to the multidisciplinary team's patient record keeping. *Figure 8.1* identifies the many facets of the nurse's many roles and responsibilities relating to record keeping.

Activity
1. Records and record keeping might relate to each of the following ethical principles, how? and why? Some of the answers may also be found in the Code (NMC, 2015).
2. Paper or computerised records: consider Thiroux and Krasemann's (2007) principles in the light of types of records you are using in your working environment
Look at the principles below and decide which aspects of record keeping would be linked to each principle. There are no absolute right and wrong answers. These principles will give you an opportunity to think, for example, 'How do I value patient X in my clinical area when I am administering their medication?' OR 'How do I tell the truth about ....?'
Value of life:
Goodness or rightness:
Truth telling or honesty:
Justice or fairness:
Autonomy, individual freedom:

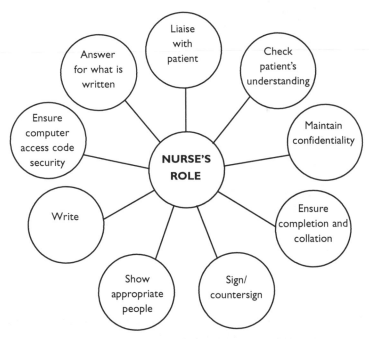

Figure 8.1. Facets of the nurse's role within record keeping.

Activity
- Think of different records that might be included in a patient's nursing records.
- Items such as prescription sheet, fluid balance chart, pressure ulcer indicator, record and pain assessment chart could be included.

Legal aspects of written and computerised communication

The two main areas of law covered here concern confidentiality of written and computerised communication and how and when this may be breached, and the security, protection and access of data. With an ever-increasing number of health professionals requiring access to information about a patient, maintaining confidentiality has become more complex. The principles of confidentiality apply equally to verbal information, manually written and computerised records.

The law recognises that confidentiality is not absolute (Dimond, 2015); nursing records may be required by a court as evidence in negligence cases, for example. In addition, the Audit Commission studies records within hospitals and makes recommendations for improvement of the quality of such records to help defend negligence claims. Courts take the view that if an action has not been recorded it has not been performed.

Confidentiality is closely associated with negligence and forms part of the duty of care of the health professional, including nurses. A legal duty exists in both common law and statutory law to maintain confidentiality. Disclosure of written information, without patient consent, is only allowed in certain circumstances.

Activity
Use the following website and associated links to determine:-
1. Who has a legal right of access to records and the process involved?
2. Under what circumstances this may be denied
3. Additional laws that could be invoked to compulsorily disclose information
www.england.nhs.uk/wp-content/uploads/2013/06/conf-policy-1.pdf
(NHS England 2014 sections 3, 4,and 8)

In many situations, if asked, patients will give consent to disclosure and sharing of written records which will enhance their care and treatment without recourse to the law. Without the consent of the patient, there may be justifiable reasons to breach confidentiality when it is in the patient's best interests, for example, to prevent harm occurring to the patient (Dimond, 2015). These circumstances are closely linked to the professional and ethical reasons discussed elsewhere in this chapter. Where information is required about a patient, but consent has not been given, or the patient is incapacitated and cannot give consent, then Section 60 of the Health and Social Care Act 2001 (now Section 251 of the NHS Act 2006) enable the use of confidential information without breaking the law (www.hra.nhs.uk).

Caldicott guardians

Each NHS organisation has an appointed Caldicott guardian who is responsible for overseeing the use and sharing of patient-based information ensuring that this is for a justifiable purpose, with only the minimum necessary information released.

Activity

Access a copy of the Caldicott Report to establish its key principles in relation to the release of patient-identifiable information.

Legally, there are instances when disclosure is compulsory. The Acts concerned include:

- The Road Traffic Act 1988 where details have to be given to the police if personal injuries or death occur.
- Prevention of Terrorism Act 1989/Anti-Terrorism, Crime and Security Act 2001 where injuries occur which may be a result of terrorist activities and there is reason to believe that an act has taken place or is likely to take place.
- Public Health (Control of Disease) Act 1984 requires personal details to be provided to the district medical officer where notifiable diseases, such as cholera, smallpox, typhus or food poisoning, are suspected.
- Police and Criminal Evidence Act 1984 enables the police to apply for powers via a judge to obtain access to material that is otherwise excluded from this legislation, such as personal records, which are confidential.
- Abortion Act 1967 requires doctors to inform the Chief Medical Officer or the Department of Health about the termination of pregnancy.

Powers of the court

Additionally, a court has the power to order documentary evidence to be provided as well as requiring a health-care professional to attend as a witness. This is known as a subpoena and it is in the interests of justice. There are some exceptions to these powers, which include issues of national security or legal privilege. However, legal privilege does not extend to nurses.

Public interest

Breach of confidentiality may be justified if it is in the public interest, defined as the interests of an individual, groups of people or society as a whole (NMC, 2015). A serious crime may be suspected, for example rape or child abuse, or an individual or groups of individuals may be at risk if someone else's health problem is not revealed. Dimond (2015) discusses the problems of public interest as there is very little guidance from the courts, apart from the American case of *Tarasoff v Regents of University of California* in 1976, and *W v Edgell* [1990]. In this latter case, an independent psychiatric report was passed to the Medical Director of W's hospital and a copy was forwarded to the Home Secretary. The psychiatrist believed the Home Office should be aware of the patient's mental health state.

This is just a brief summary of some of the legal issues surrounding confidentiality and it is unlikely that any individual nurse will be required to make decisions in relation to them alone. The onus for decision making is more often on the doctor. Other members of the health-care team, including nurses, may either be the first to be aware of potential conflicts or be party to the decision to breach confidentiality. Of course, the nurse has to deal with the patient and the consequences of such breaches in a professional and sensitive manner.

There is also legislation that relates to security of, and access to information. The main acts are summarised below and you are asked to think about some of the implications for nurses.

Computer Misuse Act 1990

This broad act aims to combat various forms of deliberate misuse (including 'hacking') which are of public concern. As there is increasing use being made of computerised record systems in all areas of health care, the nurse needs to know the key aspects.

The main offences are:

- Unauthorised access or intent to access, or to make a computer perform a function, which may enable access to an unauthorised person
- Helping someone else commit an offence
- Unauthorised modification of contents which may impair computer operation, prevent/hinder access to data or impair the reliability of data.

In other words, this means a deliberate attempt to do something that affects the way a computer works or changes something the computer has recorded so that it affects the information it contains in some way.

If any of these offences are committed and the person is found guilty, a 6-month prison sentence and/or fine may be imposed.

This sounds very technical and worrying for those dealing with computerised data, but the purpose is to protect individuals who have confidential information stored on computers. Nurses must ensure that their practice does not allow anyone without appropriate permission to have access to a patient's personal information.

Activity

Find out how patient information is safeguarded in your clinical practice area.

Access to Medical Reports Act 1988

This legislation enables patients to access medical reports written for insurance or employment purposes. The patient must be told a report is being asked for, give permission and be given the opportunity to see it before it is submitted. If anything is incorrect the patient is allowed to amend the report.

Activity

How might the Medical Reports Act apply to you?
Are there any exceptions to accessing such reports and under which circumstances?

Data Protection Act 1998

This law is an amalgamation of the previous Data Protection Act 1984 and the Access to Health Records Act 1990, most of which it replaces. Like the

Computer Misuse Act 1990 it aims to protect individuals from the misuse of personal information (Hendrick, 2000: 106). The act sets a similar standard to that determined by the Code (NMC, 2015) in that, for example, data should be accurate, secure and confidential.

Under the Data Protection Act patients can now apply to see both computerised and hand-written information about them irrespective of how far back the record was made. Earlier legislation restricted manual record access to records written after 1 November 1991. Access is requested in writing by the patient to either the person who made the record or, in the case of an institution such as a hospital, to the data controller who consults with the professional who made the record. A maximum £50.00 fee can be charged.

Activity
- List what you think could be the reasons for access.
- Inspection, explanation, copy, correction are some suggestions to help you.

Access applies to the patient, a person with written authorisation, a person having responsibility for a child (where the patient is the child), or a person appointed by the court (for incompetent patients).

Access is not absolute as it can be denied or restricted if there is a risk of physical or mental harm to patients as a result of letting them see their records. There are also restrictions imposed if another person mentioned in the record refuses consent or may be harmed as a result of disclosure (Dimond, 2015). Under the Freedom of Information Act 2000 members of the public can also access information held about them by public authorities (Dimond, 2015).

Activity
Make some notes on the implications of the Data Protection Act for the nurse. Identify some specific types of situations which you think could arise where access might be denied.

As mentioned earlier, record keeping often comes under scrutiny in negligence cases and patient complaints. Most problems occur through failure in basic communication, such as poor record keeping and not passing on enough information. Nurses should develop more reflective practice and keep up-to-date by reading professional literature to help heighten awareness of recurring problems.

Ethical aspects of written communication

Thiroux and Krasemann's (2007) principles relating to ethics were discussed in Section 1. These will now be related to written records.

Value of life

When you are making clinical records it is important that the task is taken seriously. This is difficult in a busy environment, with lots of distractions, so to value the life of the person you are writing about is a way to focus on the task in hand.

Look at the Code (NMC, 2015) Standard 1:1-5

If people are anxious, they sometimes come across as being rude, and a nurse needs to remember this and not make unwise judgments; by 'labelling' a patient, that nurse removes that person's individuality.

Some laws and ways of communicating effectively have been discussed in this book and it would be good if you could apply these theories and some of the ideas to enable you to increase the value of the life of the individual you are caring for.

Confidentiality is the key word, and this must also be respected if using one of your patients as a case study, or reflecting on a critical incident. It is important that you gain the consent of the person, but still change all the details. The Code (NMC, 2015) Standard 5.1-5.5.

Goodness or rightness

Records are written and maintained for the continuity of care for an individual. This is why they always need to be accurate and clear, so that the subsequent readers can do the most good (beneficence). It would be unethical to show a record (which would contain personal information) to anyone who asked. There is always a need to check on the individual's 'need to know'. The notion of confidentiality is based on this principle. Refer to the Code (NMC, 2015) as above.

Truth-telling and honesty

Truth-telling and honesty are highly relevant. When writing records it is essential to tell the truth and use the most appropriate words; consider the consequences of using the wrong words.

In the truth-telling context, you would need to make sure that patients understand what is happening or is going to happen to them and the possible consequences of the procedure. If patients are unsure, you need to work in partnership with people to make sure you deliver care effectively. The Code (NMC, 2015) Standards 2.1, 2.4, 2.6.

Justice and fairness

It is in patients' best interests that they have the option to contribute to the care that they receive and it is only fair that they can have the opportunity to see documents and have these explained to them. This has been discussed in the legal aspects of communication part of this chapter.

Activity

Think of an example where similar words, or spellings of words, could convey different meanings. Also see the Code (NMC, 2015) Standard 10.1-6

Autonomy, individual freedom

All the examples given above which relate to patients being involved in their records and the keeping of their records imply that there is the opportunity for choice. The patient may choose to let professional staff advise them rather than to question them. The patient's wishes must be honoured.

You will also need to consider the patient's autonomy when writing records as the patient can challenge what you have written and then you will have to justify your actions, in other words, be accountable. In some circumstances, a patient may personally contribute to the records. For example many GP surgeries operate an online system where patients can (after registering for online access) choose their appointment time, review and comment about their digitalised medical notes; some GP services operate a face-to-face online consultation service which is particularly empowering for patients who are housebound or who have limited transportation options. Details and guidance about the Patient Online initiatives are available at the NHS England website.

Activity

Think of any examples where you have seen a patient personally contributing to a record. How did this work with electronic records?

This chapter concludes with an alphabetical chart (see below) as a reminder of all the different factors which need to be in place for records and record keeping.

Useful facts about records and record keeping

Sometimes it is easier to remember facts if they are put in an unusual format. Using the alphabet, here are some facts to remember about records and record keeping:

A   Nurses are Accountable for the patient's records and should Avoid Abbreviations.

B   Handwritten records must be written in Black ink.

C   Must be Correct, Current, Comprehensive, Chronological, Consistent, Clear, Countersigned, Confidential, and Computerised.

D   Should be Detailed and Dated, and computerised information not Deleted.

E   Can be used as Evidence.

F   Must be written Factually.

G   Can be Given to the patient under the Data Protection Act 1998.

H   Must be Honest; and legible when Hand written.

I   Must Involve the patient, carers and significant others.

J   Must be Judgement free.

K   Need to be Kept for varying periods of time, e.g. adults and children.

L   Need to be Legible and Literate and are a Legal requirement.

M   Should be Meaningful and useful to the Multidisciplinary personnel who read them.

N   No-one should make any derogatory comments.

O   Should be Objective.

P   Suitable for Printing or Photocopying, Password Protect.

Q   Should Question your practice for improvements when necessary.

R   Demonstrate your Rationale for care delivery.

S   Must be Secure Signed Safeguarding computer access.

T   Must be Timed and dated.

U   Should be Unaltered and Unable to be amended electronically.

V   Should be Verifiable and Valid.

W   'If it has not been Written (recorded) it has not been done.'

X   No mistakes, but if there are, they need to be crossed through (X) and signed.

Y   Always ask, 'WhY am I writing this record?' 'Who is going to read it?'

Z   Be Zealous for excellence.

References

Dimond B (2015) *Legal aspects of nursing.* 7th edn. Pearson Education, Harlow

Hendrick J (2000) *Law and Ethics in Nursing and Health Care.* Stanley Thornes, Cheltenham

Nursing and Midwifery Council (2015) *The Code: Professional standards of practice and behaviour for nurses and midwives.* Nursing and Midwifery Council, London

Tarasoff v *Regents of University of California 17* Cal 3d 425 (1976) (USA)

Thiroux J, Krasemann KW (2007) *Ethics: Theory and practice* (9th edn). Prentice Hall, New Jersey

W v Edgell [1990] 1 All ER 835 and 1 All ER 855CA

Websites

Action on Elder Abuse: *www.elderabuse.co.uk*

Age UK: *www.ageuk.org.uk*

Audit Commission: *www.audit-commission.gov.uk*

British and Irish Legal Information Institute: *www.bailii.org*

Carers UK: *www.carersuk.org*

Care Quality Commission: *www.cqc.org.uk*

Department for Children, Schools and Families (Children Act 2004 guidance): *www.dcsf.gov.uk/everychildmatters*

Department of Education: Safeguarding and Social Work Reform guidelines: *www.education.gov.uk*

Department of Health: *www.dh.gov.uk*

General Medical Council: *www.gmc-uk.org*

Health and Safety Executive: *www.hse.gov.uk*

HM Courts Service: *www.hmcourts-service.gov.uk*

Independent Safeguarding Authority: *www.isa-gov.org.uk/*

Legislation – Government legislation: *www.legislation.gov.uk*

Medical Protection Society has good advice about gaining consent from children *www.medicalprotection.org*

MENCAP (learning disabilities charity): *www.mencap.org.uk*

Mind (mental health charity): *www.mind.org.uk*

National Audit Office: *www.nao.org.uk*

NHS Evidence- has a large data base of standards and guidelines: *www.library.nhs.uk*

NHS Litigation Authority: *www.nhsla.com*

Nursing and Midwifery Council: *www.nmc-uk.org/*

National Society for the Prevention of Cruelty to Children: *www.nspcc.org.uk*

Scottish Government: *www.scotland.gov.uk*

Appendix

The following questions may help you to pull together many of the strands that have been identified in this book. They are designed to help you to consider the different issues that have been presented and hopefully will help you see how the legal, ethical and professional issues affect your day-to-day practice as a nurse, whether you are a student or qualified.

Question 1

Using the NMC Code (NMC, 2015) and the concept of confidentiality discuss the legal, ethical and professional issues a student nurse should consider when making an entry in a patient record.

Question 2

Consent, truth-telling and autonomy are vital factors to consider when undertaking patient care. Discuss the legal, ethical and professional implications of these factors when you are delivering care to a patient in your area of practice.

References

Nursing and Midwifery Council (2015) *The Code: Professional standards of practice and behavior for nurses and midwives*. Nursing and Midwifery Council, London

Index